Miracle WARRIOR

Surviving a Shattered Life

BY

GIGI CRAMER

with

Christina M. Cavitt & Geni Cavitt

Library of Congress Control Number: 2021918863
ISBN - 978-1-662-92235-0

. . . . .

Table of Contents

PART II: WHAT'S IT LIKE TO DIE?

Dedication

Mother taught me nearly everything I needed to know about life:

1. If you see someone without a smile, give them one of yours;
2. A stranger is a friend you haven't met yet; and
3. Pay it forward by giving back and leave the world better than before you arrived.

She was a phenomenal pediatric pathologist, a feminist before her time, a medical visionary and a fabulous single parent. She was my first advocate, a Southern lady and a steel magnolia.

I dedicate the following pages to the memory of Mother, Dr. Grace Cornelia Hughes Guin. She was my heroine. I also dedicate this manuscript to both my sons, Randall and Cameron, without whom there would be no book.

- Gigi Cramer

Introduction

"Oh, my God, Sweetheart, we're going to die!" And we did.

It was Super Bowl Sunday, February 1, 2015.

Little did I know those would be the last words I would utter before my life changed forever and the last I would say to my dear husband. So began a journey of pain, loss, anger, depression, fear, addiction, faith, gratitude, forgiveness, revelation, resilience and recovery.

My husband of 22 years, Edward, had been at the wheel, navigating us home to San Diego from a wonderful but exhausting real estate conference in Palm Springs. I was dozing off in the passenger seat as we neared the end of our journey. Suddenly, I felt our car speeding up, going faster and faster! My eyes shot open as I realized we were careening down the offramp at Mira Mesa Boulevard and then barreling over four lanes of traffic. I looked at Ed. He had suddenly slumped over the steering wheel. I screamed as we slammed into a 35-foot steel traffic pole at 70 miles an hour.

I survived. He did not.

You'll hear more about this tragedy in the second half of my story. For now, I'll simply say the accident changed my life, and, in some ways, redefined me. But that single event isn't who I am, nor exclusively what this book is about. Rather, herein is my tale of History and Hope. Tragedy and Survival. Drama and Humor. Recovery and Thriving. And my precious family and friends who have made life worth living.

Stick with me, dear reader. Buckle up. It's quite a ride.

Before I Died
PART I

"Nil Desperandum"

[Never despair, never give up.]

Latin motto

CHAPTER 1

The Original Coal Miner's Daughter

In the spring of 1912, the magnificent RMS Titanic collided with a giant iceberg in the North Atlantic and sank. That same year, three months after this horrific collision at sea, a little girl was born in Birmingham, Alabama. She was the first child of Grace Hawkins Hughes and Ernest Sutton Hughes. They named her Grace Cornelia. Later, her baby brother, Ernest Jr., arrived, completing the little family and living together in a cramped mining town row house.

The famous country song depicting the life of coal miners (see excerpt at right) describes my grandfather's plight toiling in Birmingham's subterranean landscape. Always dangerous and often deadly, it was a miserable way to eke out a living. But he was stuck due, in no small part to his selfish, lazy wife, who spent his meager earnings on frivolity – silly hats, fancy dresses and unnecessary domestic help.

Despite the hardships, my grandfather, Earnest, was a proud, dyed-in-the-wool coal miner. Unfortunately, back then, there was no OSHA and precious few miner safety mechanisms in place. Sure, they used helmets and flashlights, and had caged canaries to detect odorless but deadly gas. Whenever one of those little birds keeled over, my grandfather and his buddies ran like hell to escape the fumes. Other than that, masks were unheard of and the big bosses weren't worried about air quality deep underground. If a man quit or was killed, there was always another victim standing in line to get his job.

> ## "I Owe My Soul to the Company Store"
>
> lyrics from Merle Travis's Sixteen Tons,
> made famous by Tennessee Ernie Ford
>
> Some people say a man is made outta mud
> A poor man's made outta muscle and blood
> Muscle and blood and skin and bones
> A mind that's a-weak and a back that's strong
> You load sixteen tons, what do you get?
> Another day older and deeper in debt
> Saint Peter don't you call me 'cause I can't go
> I owe my soul to the company store

The coal was bituminous – black, viscous and oily. Performing backbreaking labor over long shifts, my grandfather inhaled poison thousands of times a day. He died way too young of black lung disease. But that's getting ahead of the story. While my grandfather labored, his spendthrift wife continued her ways. Of course, she needed a new frock and frilly hat every Easter. She wanted the finest of everything, but my grandfather couldn't afford it. An additional expense was my grandmother hiring someone to clean the house. Unfortunately, that domestic helper had contracted tuberculosis – then called consumption – and trudged throughout the house tending to her various chores, coughing everywhere until she became so sick that she had to quit working for the Hughes family. But not before she passed the illness along to Mother.

Mother loved school and was good at all her subjects, especially chemistry and physiology. She went to Birmingham Southern College and graduated *magna cum laude*. After she graduated, her grandparents visited Birmingham from Kentucky. While sitting on the front porch, sipping on their lovely mint juleps, my great-grandmother, Grace Hawkins, fixed her gaze on Mother to ask, "Little Grace, what would you like to do, now that you've graduated from college?" To which my mother responded, "You know what I really want to do? I want to go to medical school."

Bituminous coal - my grandfather's life and death

Before my great-grandmother had time to react to the young woman's words, my grandmother inserted, "Now Grace, you understand we've had this conversation before. There's absolutely no money to send you to medical school. All you have to do now is marry one of these coal miner boys, stay at home and have a passel of kids. And you will just be the most educated mama in the world."

Indignant, my great-grandmother slammed down her walking cane, turned to my great-grandfather and said, "Mr. Hawkins, when we get back to Lexington, I want you to cash in our World War (pronounced Woe-Wa) bonds. We are going to send our gal to medical school."

For the record, my ancestors all spoke with thick southern accents. For instance, when I was a child, Mother read me Bible stories like Noah and the Ark. I said that I knew other boys' names, but I never heard of the name Noah. Mother smiled and said, "Darlin', it's Noah. N-O-A-H. It rhymes with "Do-ah. D-O-O-R." You can't make this up.

After the heated discussion on the front porch, my great-grandparents returned to Kentucky and cashed in their "woe-wa" bonds to ensure there was cash for Mother to go to medical school. Sadly, before they had time to return with the funds, Mother came down with consumption. To add to the misfortune, two of Mother's close girlfriends, who were regulars at the Hughes' house, got sick, too.

At the time, there was no real treatment for this lung ailment and the wisdom of the day dictated that the afflicted spend time outside. The experts, such as they were, felt patients had a better chance for survival with a regiment of fresh air. So Mother and her two friends were shipped off to Tennessee, all the way up to the very top of the Great Smoky Mountains, to convalesce in a sanatorium. Their beds were located in a large outdoor porch known as the Widow's Walk. The spring, summer and fall were tolerable. Winter, however, was bitterly cold.

Weeks went by, then months. Mother became worse and worse. She lost both of her girlfriends. But Mother was a true steel magnolia and she hung on. My grandmother visited her, bringing magazines and newspapers to satisfy my mother's voracious appetite for reading. After Mother devoured the contents, she folded up the newspapers and magazines, and tucked them around her for insulation. Years later, when she and I strolled the Tidal Basin for the Washington, D.C. annual Cherry Blossom Festival, she would remark at the homeless on the park benches, "That's the way I used to keep warm back at the sanatorium, using papers as insulation." I have no idea why all the tuberculosis patients in the 1930s Deep South were forced outside year around. Apparently, the medical wisdom was, "What doesn't kill you only makes you stronger."

By the way, even though I'm not a fan of early mornings, getting up at 5 a.m. with my mother and going to the Cherry Blossom Festival every spring counts among my fondest memories.

Alexander Fleming's miracle

Mother was fascinated by any and all medical literature. One particularly frigid afternoon in the sanatorium, she came across an article about a Scottish physician and microbiologist named Sir Alexander Fleming, credited with discovering penicillin. But since penicillin had not yet received U.S. government approval, it was not available to the general public. In fact, the only way to acquire the drug was on the black market.

In a fit of uncharacteristic selflessness, my grandmother sought out resources in the unsavory parts of Birmingham to sell her wedding ring and use the proceeds to illegally procure enough penicillin to help my mother. Mother started treating herself and over the next 18 months, she unpredictably got better.

The doctors who visited her on a regular basis noticed that her health was improving. But she didn't tell about her self-administered treatment and they didn't ask. Those physicians simply remarked on her returning good health and attributed it to their brilliant care. After three years in the sanatorium, Mother was finally discharged. Soon after she returned to Birmingham, she contacted her grandparents and they sent her their World War savings bonds money.

It was 1939. Mother had the gumption, drive and perseverance, and thanks to her grandparents, enough money to fulfill her dreams.

CHAPTER 2

I Am Here to Become a Physician

In the spring of 1940, Mother purchased a fashionable new flowered dress, packed up an old valise and took the Southern Railway to Nashville, Tennessee, where she made her way to the Vanderbilt University School of Medicine. She walked in the front door, found out where the dean of admissions was located and marched into his office.

"Hello," she demanded, more than greeted.

"Do you have an appointment?" Responded the self-important man behind the big mahogany desk.

"No, I do not."

"Well, little lady. How might I help you?"

"I am here to become a physician."

"Ma'am, we're training doctors here. You gotta go down yonder, to the other end of Nashville, directly to the School of Nursing. That's where you belong."

Early portrait of Grace Hughes

This was the wrong thing to say to Mother, who had fought desperate illness and medical ignorance for years to finally arrive at Vanderbilt. Standing straight to her full height of 5' 9", she politely but directly reiterated, "No, actually, I am here to become a physician."

Not to be outdone by a mere female, the dean explained with exaggerated patience, "Ma'am, again, we're training doctors. Male doctors. We allowed a woman into the school a couple years back. Yeah, she was

Vanderbilt University School of Medicine, 1943.
Photograph used by permission from Vanderbilt University.

coming not for an M.D., but an 'MRS.' She had the gall to replace one of our fine young male applicants, but ended up quitting when she took one of our graduates to the altar. Our resources were wasted on her."

Mother, never losing her cool, demurred, "I understand what you're saying, sir. But I need to let you know that there are no rules and regulations that prevent women from entering your medical program. I am here to become a physician, and by God, I am going to become an M.D. at Vanderbilt medical school."

Well, nobody liked it, but she got in and proved herself to be exceptional, particularly in determining causes of death. When called upon during autopsies, she would examine the cadaver and in short order, accurately identify what ended that person's life.

The men loathed her. She messed up their "good-old-boy network" that had been doing just fine for all those decades without a woman. They hated her because she was so bright and knew exactly what she needed to do to be successful. Initially, she wanted to be an obstetrician, but changed her mind.

"You know, Darlin'," she told me. "I changed fields because my pathology patients would never call me at 2 a.m. to attend a birth."

She burned the midnight oil hour after hour after hour. She did everything in her power to become her absolute best. She studied with and spoke to interns. She did all the required grand rounds, where the unique diagnoses of patients were discussed among physicians, pharmacists and students. Sometimes, the medical students would follow the grand rounds tours for 30 hours straight.

In addition to the grueling work of the program, Mother was subject to no end of shenanigans and downright bullying from her colleagues. For instance, to save money, she always packed a brown paper bag lunch of an economical peanut butter and jelly sandwich, an apple and a little carton of milk. She put her name on the bag and placed it in the physicians' lounge refrigerator. After an exhausting grand rounds, when she was almost too weak to walk, she would retire to the lounge and open the refrigerator door to grab her lunch bag.

The first time she did this, the bag felt too light. She opened it and there was nothing left except the crust from her sandwich, an empty milk carton and an apple core. On a little paper napkin that she had included with her lunch was written, "Thanks, Doc. Lunch was terrific."

Mother tolerated this harassment for about two weeks. Then she realized she was getting pretty hungry because she was missing her midday meal. There was a cafeteria, but that cost money she didn't have. Even though her grandparents had provided funds for medical school, there was very little left over to pay for food.

Finally, enough was enough. Mom devised a plan, leveraging the physician's lounge entrance and exit. To facilitate privacy, lounge access featured two doors, an inner door and a few steps further, an outer door leading into the corridor. That day, Mother taped a poster on the outer exit door so medical school personnel couldn't possibly miss it when they left the lounge.

As the male students walked in one afternoon, they helped themselves to Mother's precious lunch bag. And as they were leaving, they couldn't help but see Mother's poster: "Congratulations, gentlemen, you have just consumed the milk of one of my syphilitic patients." And that was the last time they ever touched Mother's lunch.

'A date which will live in infamy'

December 7, 1941, was what President Franklin D. Roosevelt dubbed, "a date which will live in infamy." That's when Japanese forces bombed Pearl Harbor and awakened the sleeping giant that was the United States' powerful military. It marked the beginning of U.S. involvement in World War II and thrust the country's entire medical curriculum into an accelerated mode. At Vanderbilt Medical School, every man and one singular woman – Mother – were compelled to complete their studies as quickly as possible.

1943 graduating class of Vanderbilt School of Medicine

Forget taking summers off. They worked around the clock to earn their degrees and begin working as doctors for the war effort.

Mother graduated near Christmas, 1943. Then she went home, planning to get down to work as a full-fledged doctor. The social bias of the time, and fate, had other plans.

CHAPTER 3

The Dashing Young Officer

With her newly-minted M.D. diploma in hand, Mother returned to Birmingham in January, 1944. One fine Sunday morning, she attended services at Birmingham Christian Church. She and her family situated themselves on a pew near the front. Then, in walked a U.S. Air Force colonel. He slid into a seat directly across from them.

Mother was bedazzled. Never in her young life had she seen the likes of this – a dashing young officer, resplendent in his immaculate dress uniform, shiny silver buttons, elegant rank stripes and impeccably polished shoes. Remember, this was coal country. She was used to the grimy brown jackets, dirty footwear and oil-stained overalls of the miners. The men populating the pews and church socials, even decked out in their Sunday best, never captured Mother's attention, much less her heart. This fellow was a different story entirely.

When the organist pounded out the prelude and the choir joined in, Mother heard nary a note. She was utterly distracted by the debonair figure in her peripheral vision. Of course, Southern ladies never outright stared, although she wanted to. The service dragged on endlessly, but finally, the preacher called for the closing hymn and the congregation migrated to the church yard where the pair were properly introduced. Back then, there were strict rituals between young men and women who were drawn to one another. A formal introduction was required, preferably by the parents of the parties. My grandmother and the officer's aunt knew one another, so they did the honors.

"How do you do?" Colonel Joel Brown Guin queried, gallantly taking Mother's hand and making the slightest bow. She nearly fainted, but maintained her composure.

"I do very well," she responded in her genteel Southern drawl. "What brings you to our fine city?" She learned that Joel Guin had taken the train from Maxwell Field in Montgomery, Alabama, to Birmingham for the weekend to visit his aunt and uncle.

You may have noticed that while this man would become my biological parent, I rarely refer to him as "my father." You see, it turned out that Mother's flyboy was a fly-by-night scoundrel.

In short order, the airman swept her off her feet and she fell madly in love. Of course, my grandparents disapproved of him. Maybe they detected something unsavory in the man that their daughter was too smitten to notice. In any case, he was clearly not a local and in the tightly knit coal community, all outsiders were suspect.

Despite everything else, after a whirlwind courtship, the young couple wed in the spring of 1944. Then he whisked her off to Washington, D.C., where he had been reassigned to the U.S. Pentagon.

A year later, in the fall, I was born. Three months premature!

CHAPTER 4

Greatest Generation to Baby Boomers

I was among the first of the generation to be dubbed Baby Boomers. We are the children of the "Greatest Generation" who fought in World War II. Mother could only carry me for six months because she was dying of toxemia (now called eclampsia). It became very clear she needed an emergency Caesarian section, which meant I was going to make an early appearance. Just before the procedure, she had the knowledge and presence of mind to assert, "Under no circumstances are you to give my baby extra oxygen."

Her obstetrician did not understand why she would make such a wild demand. After all, I arrived weighing just three pounds. He insisted, "Dr. Guin, she's got to have oxygen. She is so little. It will get her lungs developing much faster and get her out of the 'premie' incubator earlier." Mother repeated, "Absolutely no oxygen for my daughter!" He may not have completely understood, but thankfully, he obeyed her.

Mother knew what, evidently, the attending physician didn't – that too much oxygen in a premature infant would increase a tiny baby's susceptibility to retinopathy of prematurity (ROP), a condition which could have blinded me for life. In fact, there are Boomers walking around today with white canes because they were premies in the 1940s and force-fed too much oxygen.

Once again, Mother was way ahead of her time.

Daddy bolts

For the first two years of my life, Mother and I lived in the Washington, D.C. area while my biological father, an Army Air Force colonel, worked in matters of national security at the Pentagon. After my second birthday, my so-called "father" came home and left a note on the pillow in the master bedroom. The coward had scribbled this short missive: "I no longer want to be married, and I sure as hell don't want a kid." He went on to write that he was going back to New York to attend NYU to earn his Master's of Business Administration.

This was a staggering blow to Mother. She was still in love with him and devoted to her baby. She could hardly understand what had just happened. But there she was, alone and on her own.

As a pathologist in Washington, one would have thought that she was a well-respected, gainfully employed physician. But in the late 1940s, there were few female doctors practicing medicine anywhere across the country. Infuriatingly, women were regarded as less important and less capable than their male counterparts. Without the colonel's income, she was financially strapped, but remained steadfast in her care for me. Unfortunately, he left us with nothing and couldn't be bothered to ever provide child support.

A year following my father's desertion and after a great deal of soul searching, Mother got a divorce. It wasn't long before she came to the realization that she needed additional training and more experience if she was going to hold down a practice and adequately provide for her daughter. She was passionate about pediatric leukemia and eradicating childhood cancer, an arena requiring highly specialized education. Fortunately, among her many attributes, and paramount to her success in life, she was a relentless fact-finder. Her rigorous research indicated the best place for her

Memorial Sloan Kettering Cancer Center today

19

to acquire that specialized training was at Memorial Sloan Kettering Cancer Center, New York City's renowned research center.

Mother requested an appointment with the pediatric research team. She applied, and wonder of wonders, was accepted on their staff. Her pathology credentials were precisely what they were looking for. She was the only female physician, but after a fashion, her colleagues begrudgingly seemed to accept her. As a brain trust, these physicians discovered that when the steroid cortisone was injected into pediatric leukemia patients, the result could add years to a child's life. This breakthrough was significant. Mother wrote articles about their findings for medical journals that were translated worldwide.

What to do with the baby?

In order to move to New York City to take this job, Mother had one huge problem to overcome. Me. Oh, she didn't see me as a problem. She loved me completely. But she realized that as the newest physician on staff, her hours would be long, late and grueling. How could she possibly take care of a toddler? She had to leave me with somebody. But whom? And how? And where?

Fortunately, during her time in Washington, D.C., Mother had become friends with a woman named Franny Yowell, who ran an early daycare center out of her home in Arlington, Virginia. Daycare as a recognized business was a newish concept in the late 1940s, but I required overnight care, too, so it was a pretty big deal. Mother and Mrs. Yowell talked over the telephone and met in person. Her familiarity with Mrs. Yowell helped her feel more secure leaving me in this woman's care. Still, knowing Mother, it must have been excruciatingly painful for her to leave her baby girl behind.

Guardian: large and in charge

Mrs. Yowell was a dynamic whirlwind who ran her household with a certain efficiency. She was kind enough to me, but had three children of her own, all older than I, who demanded a good deal of her energy. I have vague, mostly happy memories of that time. Yet there were difficulties. I lived with the

Yowells for three and a half years, sleeping in the basement, alone, in a single bed. I had a few toys, a bookshelf with books for little people and a couple of chairs. I recall feeling lonely most of the time and a little scared living alone in that basement.

I suffered from all kinds of allergies and asthma, so most of my activities were confined to the house. I distinctly remember wanting to play outside with her children – especially when it snowed – but I could only venture into the yard when it was warm. So during winter and inclement weather, I stood on a big box in my basement bedroom and watched longingly through the window at all of the other kids having a marvelous time playing in the snow. I was only able to experience those white fluffy snowflakes on my way to or coming home from kindergarten.

Gigi, circa 1948, in Mrs. Yowell's back yard.

Twice a month, from Friday night to Sunday afternoon, Mother rescued me from my loneliness.

"Your Dr. Guin is coming home to visit," Mrs. Yowell would declare every other Friday. At first, I had no idea who this Dr. Guin was. I was too little to really understand that I lived in one place and my mommy was someplace else. After all, Mrs. Yowell took care of me, fed me, bathed me, played with me – she acted like my mother. But she wasn't. Evidently, though, I inherently knew who Mother was and when "My Dr. Guin" arrived at the house, I felt a deep sense of security and love.

Without fail, every other weekend, Mother made the four-hour journey to be with me. She took the subway from Memorial Sloan Kettering to Grand Central Station where she boarded a train for the long trek to Union Station in Washington, D.C. Then she hopped on two different street cars and a bus to get out to Arlington, Virginia, near Clarendon.

Because Mother left after her shift on Fridays, it could be as late as 10 p.m. before she arrived at the Yowells'. On those evenings, I was allowed to stay up late. I attribute that happy late night anticipation as one of the reasons I became such a night owl. When she arrived, "Dr. Guin" would come downstairs, throw her arms around me and we would sprawl out on my 3/4 size bed (larger than a single, but smaller than a double) with her suitcase full of books and toys. Pretty soon, I'd start getting sleepy, so she and I would crawl under the covers and she read me stories, and told funny little tales about what she was doing up in the big city of New York.

I came to love every other Friday night, knowing that this incredible lady would come through the door with a suitcase of presents for me. Twice a month, it was like Christmas.

Gunny Ratty

On my third birthday, Mother brought me a stuffed animal. It was a beautifully plush gray and white bunny rabbit that was as tall as I was. I couldn't say, "bunny rabbit" because the words were too big, so I called him "Gunny Ratty." That little rabbit would be one of my best friends until I left to go to the College of William and Mary 15 years later. Gunny Ratty was always there, even if "My Dr. Guin" wasn't. I had Gunny Ratty, and for me that meant Mother was never far away.

The day finally came that Mother took me home for good. It was one of the most exciting days of my life!

After Mother's pediatric leukemia findings were published worldwide, Dr. Georgios Papanikolaou, a Greek cytopathologist – a pathologist who studies tissue fragments to create diagnoses – read her articles and was markedly impressed. He flew to New York and called on Mother at Memorial Sloan Kettering to improvise a plan in which she was to play a critical role.

'Lie down and spread your legs'

His research was in women's health, specifically in developing a system of discovery and treatment for cervical and uterine cancer. He was establishing the United States' first women's public health clinic in Washington, D.C. After reading Mother's work, he decided that he wanted her to be the female pathologist who could credibly say, "Darlin', lie down, spread your legs and put your feet in these little old stirrups. We are going to scrape your uterine wall to check for uterine and cervical cancers."

Mother fulfilled her obligations at Memorial Sloan Kettering and began working with Dr. Papanikolaou after she returned to Washington, D.C. With her new job in the nation's capital, Mother could now afford an apartment. Moving day arrived and Mother helped me pack my things. We said good-bye to Mrs. Yowell and her family and off we drove to our new Arlington, Virginia apartment. I was over the moon with happiness. She and I were a family once again.

DR. GRACE HUGHES GUIN 1912—2002

Text based on data from Oakhill Cemetery, Birmingham, Alabama

By graduating in an otherwise all-male class at Vanderbilt University School of Medicine in 1943, Grace Hughes Guin scored a victory for feminism. Moreover, she became a world-renowned pediatric pathology physician.

In the 1950s, after a fellowship at the prestigious Sloan Kettering Memorial Cancer Center in New York, she joined Dr. George Papinacolaou, inventor of the pap smear for cancer screening, in opening a pioneering women's health clinic in Washington, D.C. She went on to publish articles in more than 50 languages about pediatric leukemia and other childhood diseases.

From 1954 to 1964, Dr. Guin was a pathologist at Children's Hospital in Washington, D.C., where she began researching the effects of cortisone treatments in pediatric leukemia. She was widely recognized for her success in prolonging the lives of young leukemia patients through intravenous cortisone treatments. Her research at Children's Hospital appeared in such publications as *The New England Journal of Medicine* and *The Journal of the American Medical Association*.

She was later appointed chief of pathology at Arlington Hospital in Virginia. In 1967, Dr. Guin was named special assistant to the director of pathology at the Veterans Administration in Washington, D.C. She oversaw more than 90 V.A.

hospitals nationwide until she retired in 1990. Upon retiring, she received the Distinguished Career Award from the Veterans Administration.

Dr. Guin was born in Birmingham. According to her daughter, Gigi, "She was always the epitome of a Southern genteel lady. She had an intense interest in medicine and her dreams came true when she was admitted into Vanderbilt Medical School. Dr. Guin was accepted into Vanderbilt after graduating Phi Beta Kappa from Birmingham Southern College. In 1991, Birmingham Southern honored her with a distinguished alumni award."

"Grace was an advocate for women in medicine at a time when there weren't many in the profession," said Dr. Enid Gilbert, a professor of pathology and pediatrics at the University of South Florida. "She was an outstanding pathologist and an astute diagnostician. I met her when I was a resident at Children's Hospital, and she influenced me into becoming a pediatrician."

Toward the end of her life, Mother requested that, on her gravestone, I would inscribe, "Mother and Physician." I asked her if it would be okay if I added a couple of adjectives – "Beloved Mother – Devoted Physician." That's what's on her gravestone at Oakhill Memorial Cemetery in Birmingham, Alabama. Half of her ashes are buried there – the other half are interred at my church in La Jolla, California where I can easily visit my beloved mother.

Gravestone of Grace Hughes Guin

CHAPTER 5

Home of Our Own – Finally!

Mother and I settled in the Colonial Village Apartments on Buckingham Street in Arlington, Virginia. She enrolled me into first grade at nearby James Monroe Elementary.

The first day of school, Mother dressed me in my best little jumper, shiny new patent leather Mary Janes and anklet socks, and then brushed my hair into a pony tail. It was pretty standard fashion for grade schoolers in the early 1950s. I wriggled and squirmed under her ministrations. I was very nervous to start my first day of school. After living in the Yowells' basement, the prospect of meeting and playing with a bunch of new kids was exciting… and terrifying.

Mama sat me down at our kitchen table the first day of school for breakfast and I stared at my food.

"Little Grace," she said. "You have to eat or you'll just faint before lunchtime!"

"Oh, Mama. I'm too excited." The truth was, I was scared to death.

James Monroe Elementary

"I understand. Now listen, here's what you do. You march right up to a girl with the kindest eyes and tell her your name. Just be yourself and she'll want to be your friend." What sound advice! I was nervous about this, but I trusted Mama, so I managed to choke down a few bites.

My elementary school parking lot was all hustle and bustle as children piled out of big yellow busses and ungainly, wood-sided station wagons. Frazzled-looking teachers were admonishing children to "settle down" and form orderly rows to enter the building. I felt comfortable as Mother took me by the hand and walked me up to a nice lady shepherding the littlest children. While the adults talked, I spied a girl who looked nice. She smiled at me and I smiled back. So I let go of Mother's hand and walked over to her.

"My name is Grace Guin," I said shyly.

"I'm Patsy," she replied. "Wanna be friends?"

"Oh, yes," I said, taking her hand as we skipped into line.

Ever watchful, Mother saw this interaction and knew I'd be okay.

From first grade through sixth, Patsy and I were best friends. A third little girl played with us, too. Her name was Lloyd. Evidently, her father expected a boy and when she was born, wanted to name her like a boy, so Lloyd she was.

School became lots more fun since I had girlfriends to study and hang around with. Mom was always there for me and loved driving me to school in her classy 1957 turquoise Chevy Bel Air.

1957 Chevrolet Bel Air

When I was 11 years old, I began to have an interest in boys. Around that time, Elvis Presley was a big deal. Now, Mother didn't like Elvis — too much hip gyration for her taste. And she didn't want me paying any attention to this young man. But girls were crazy about this new singing sensation. We didn't have money for a television, but Patsy's family had one in their recreation room and Patsy invited me over to watch him on the Ed Sullivan Show. I told Mom we were going to "study" for an exam. We may have cracked the books for a few minutes, but at 8 p.m. on September 9, 1956, we were glued to the TV, gyrating and swooning to "You Ain't Nothin' but a Hound Dog."

But it wasn't all rock 'n' roll

Despite my social life and love for rock 'n' roll, I had a serious side and I was very studious. I wanted to make the best grades possible because, although it wasn't true, I feared if I didn't make my mother proud, she'd leave me the way Daddy ditched us. Later on, I realized how irrational that thinking was. Mother loved two things in life: medicine and me. She would have to die before she'd desert me.

In 1958, I graduated into Stratford Junior High, which in 1960 was to become the first school in the Virginia Commonwealth to welcome Black students. Those young Black scholars were bussed in because Arlington, like so many cities in both the South and North, promoted segregation. But it was the early 1960s and "The Times, They Were a Changin'" (Bob Dylan, 1963). Actually, even though I was very young, I thought it was high time things changed and became equal.

The same year desegregation was taking place in our school district, Mother was now a respected forensic pathologist and had the money to buy a lovely Dutch Colonial – on a corner lot with half an acre of wooded land – at 3600 North Abingdon Street in Arlington. We finally owned our own home!

Yorktown High School

Stratford Junior High School

Freshman and sophomore years, I attended Northern Virginia's Washington and Lee High School. In 1960, my junior year, I was transferred to a brand new Yorktown High School, in Arlington County, Virginia. Since school boundaries were changed, there weren't any seniors that year, so we got to be upperclassmen two years in a row!

National City Christian Church

To teach is to learn

To hone my academic skills, I followed my mother's advice: "To teach is to learn." Consequently, I spent a lot of time tutoring arithmetic and French at the local Knights of Columbus Hall, the Shriners and several Rotary clubs. I was also very involved with our place of worship – National City Christian Church, one of the flagship Disciples of

Our Dutch Colonial home in Arlington

29

Christ Protestant churches. Every Sunday, Mother packed us off to 5 Thomas Circle in downtown D.C. I even earned a badge for perfect attendance. Remarkably, we got to see every president since Dwight D. Eisenhower grace our services, except the Catholic, John F. Kennedy. When secret service agents lined the church steps and aisles, we knew a POTUS would be present.

GUPPY LOVE

Donald Wallace was one of my mother's pediatric leukemia patients. At the time, he was 11 and I was 9. Donald's condition was terminal. The little boy bravely asserted, "I am not afraid to die. But Dr. Guin, who will take care of my fish when I'm gone?"

A compassionate doctor who truly cared about her charges, Mother knew all about the boy's passion for his collection of fantail guppies, black mollies and red swordtails. She responded, "Donald, my daughter is slightly younger than you. I'm sure she would enjoy taking care of your precious fish and always remind them how much you've adored such special 'buddies.'"

Dr. Guin and Donald

Mother came home that night and, patting my hand, explained the situation to me: "Darlin'" – as she often addressed me when imparting important information – "I have a very special and sensitive patient who is worried about who will take care of his fish after he dies. And I'm sorry to say, there's not much more I can do to extend his life this time. There is room in our tiny apartment for them. Would you be willing to take over for him?"

I was sorry to learn that a youngster close to my age was going to die. I knew how hard Mom had worked to keep him alive. Even cortisone injections had run their course and Donald was almost out of time. Mother had taught me that sometimes her young patients could not survive cancer.

"Oh, yes, Mama! Of course I will."

When Donald died, I inherited his fish. I took my new responsibilities very seriously, cleaning the tank, feeding the fish, reminding them how much Donald had cared about them, reassuring them of my love and spending hours watching my adopted aquatic buddies swim around in my new aquarium.

Thus began my love for fish and oceans.

CHAPTER 6

If It's Good Enough for Thomas Jefferson...

College of William and Mary Crest

The summer after high school, I was excited to have received acceptance from the College of William and Mary in Williamsburg, Virginia. Mother instilled in me the value and virtue of a comprehensive liberal arts education, so that's how I decided to attend the "Alma Mater of a Nation." I had been to Williamsburg several times with my mom while growing up, but I had never lived in Colonial Williamsburg. It was like going back in time 250 years. While walking up and down Duke of Gloucester Street, I encountered wardrobed characters who seemingly stepped out of the history books to engage students and curious tourists in a living conversation. George Washington, John Adams, Thomas Jefferson, Patrick Henry, Benjamin Franklin – I never knew which of these trained actors I would run across. It was not only exciting, but enlightening to engage with these colorful historical figures who created our Declaration of Independence and Constitution. These talented character actors brought history to life. They always challenged us to defend the very heart of democracy, cherishing our rights of freedom and liberty.

As a freshman, I lived in the Jefferson dorm. I mean, where else would my mother have wanted me to live? She respected highly educated, wealthy Southern gentlemen, which certainly included Thomas Jefferson.

Where there's smoke

After the first four months at college, I came home for Christmas vacation to see Mom and our lovely home in Arlington, Virginia. The first day of winter break, I invited a few friends to come over and hang out. We went into the den, gathered some soft drinks and started gabbing. I immediately discovered that while they were at college, almost every one of my girlfriends had started to smoke cigarettes. And, truth be told, I had, too. I thought it made me look very chic and sophisticated.

Bill Barker, a.k.a. Thomas Jefferson, and Gigi, taken in 2018.

As we drank our Cokes and flicked our cigarettes into the only ashtray my mother owned, I heard the upstairs door open. Footsteps hustled down the stairs. I saw the den door open, and there stood my mother. She took three long strides directly toward me, grabbed the cigarette right out of my mouth and rammed it into my soda. Without saying a word, her expression conveyed everything. She was furious. She stomped back up the stairs and into her bedroom. We all heard her door slam.

My girlfriends were just as shocked as I was and sheepishly offered feeble excuses about having to leave early. My mother was cold and distant that night, very unlike her. No words were spoken over dinner. Later in the evening, as I was getting ready for bed, my mother burst into my room to inform me she wanted me up and ready to leave the house by 7 o'clock the next morning. It was a Friday night and I wanted to sleep in on Saturday. After all, it was Christmas vacation. I complained to my mother, but she reiterated, "7 a.m.! We are out the door." I knew I was in deep trouble.

I was late getting up. Mother stormed into my room and dragged me out of bed. She demanded, "We're leaving." Not even allowing me to get dressed, she threw a robe around my shoulders and made me step into my slippers. Out the door we went.

Without a word exchanged, attired in my jammies, robe and slippers, we arrived at Arlington Hospital's back entrance. We took the elevator directly to the basement. Proceeding down a short hallway to the first door, my mother yanked her keys from her purse and put one in the lock. She opened the door, and I followed her inside.

We were in the morgue.

She got on the intercom and called an orderly. When he arrived, she asked him to open one of the refrigerated units. The orderly clicked a button. A drawer slid open and there lay a pale male corpse.

The orderly lifted the body out of the drawer, placed it on a gurney and rolled it onto the stainless steel autopsy table. Mother gripped a surgical saw. She pulled the canvas back to the waist of the corpse – a very cold, dead man. I was standing next to my mother. My stomach lurched. I decided it was time for me to desperately lower myself onto a frigid metal bench next to the morgue table. My body shook and I became increasingly nauseated as I sat there, hearing the saw tearing through the sternum of this corpse. I'll never forget the sound of ripping skin and snapping bones. Next, my mother took the forceps, inserted them into the cold chest cavity, and pulled out a shriveled, wrinkled, black mass of flesh no bigger than a pear. As she held the decayed organ tightly in the teeth of the forceps, she brought it down to my eye level and deliberately admonished, "What do you think this is?"

Judging from the position and placement of the organ in the lifeless body, I gasped, "It looks like a lung."

Mother stared pointedly at me and demanded, "Why do you think this man died?"

And I said, "He died of lung cancer." I wasn't about to say, "He fell out of a second story window." At that moment, there was no humor in her mood. None whatsoever.

Mother flatly replied, "Right again." She re-inserted the shriveled lung into the decomposing corpse, then asked the orderly to come back and return the body to the drawer.

Mother briskly led us out of the morgue, through the hospital corridors and into the light of day. Still, not a word from her. The blast of fresh air did little to mask the stench of formaldehyde and other disgusting chemical odors in my robe and as my forensic teacher-mother followed me from the morgue to the car, I remember saying to her from the depth of my fear and in profound sincerity, "Mom, you've made your point. I will never smoke again."

Life is a symphony

After Christmas break, I returned to school and found that studying for exams was nearly pleasurable at William and Mary. There, students could access the splendid gardens surrounding the Governor's Palace at the far end of Duke of Gloucester Street. Fragrant breezes from the floral gardens allowed

THE CHI OMEGA SYMPHONY

The Chi Omega Symphony is a beautifully written document that declared to Chi Omegas old and new what it meant and means to be a part of this sorority.

To live constantly above snobbery of word or deed; to place scholarship before social obligations and character before appearances; to be in the best sense, democratic rather than "exclusive," and lovable rather than "popular;" to work earnestly, to speak kindly, to act sincerely, to choose thoughtfully that course which occasion and conscience demand; to be womanly always; to be discouraged never; in a word, to be loyal under any and all circumstances to my Fraternity and her highest teachings and to have her welfare ever at heart that she may be a symphony of high purpose and helpfulness in which there is no discordant note.

Written by Ethel Switzer Howard, Xi Chapter, 1904

me to focus on my studying in a very relaxed atmosphere. The demand of preparing for those rigorous final exams was lessened by the pleasurable surroundings. Even after I closed my books, I would find every opportunity to sit on the palace benches and meditate amidst the peace these exquisite gardens offered.

In my sophomore year, I was fortunate to pledge the prestigious Chi Omega Sorority. Little did I know until I became a Sister that there were a number of well-known Chi Omegas around the country. These outstanding individuals have continuously made magnificent strides in the world of medicine, law, art, education, literature, the judicial system and politics. Notably, United States President Joe Biden appointed Jen Psaki as the White House Press Secretary — a Chi Omega from William and Mary College. I am so honored to be her sorority sister.

I am proud of the fact that one my favorite novels, *To Kill a Mockingbird*, was written by one of the most celebrated Chi Omegas, Harper Lee. To this day, I am still connected to and feel very close with many of my sorority sisters, specifically the ones in and around Virginia. As an only child, it is reassuring to know I have supportive and close relationships with quite a few Chi Omega sisters.

Collegiate sports

Golf was a popular sport with some of the college students, but chasing a little white ball for 18 holes was way too slow for this energetic co-ed. To balance out the demands of classes, studying and work, I loved swimming and enjoyed lacrosse. I also developed a passion for tennis, which would keep me active and fit for decades. I have been excited to share my love of the game with my sons. In fact, Cameron and I won several "Senior - Sprouts" doubles tournaments after he picked up the racquet. My grades were good enough to please Mother. I proudly graduated in 1966 from the College of William and Mary with a B.A. in Humanities and Fine Arts, and a minor in French. To celebrate, she took me to New York to see my very first Broadway play. *Man of LaMancha* was a big hit and the "theater bug" bit me big time! It was mesmerizing the way actors on a stage could transport audiences to other places and times. I fell madly in love with Richard Kiley, who played the lead – he was gorgeous, and what a talent! "The Impossible Dream" became my theme song, especially later on, during my bouts with breast cancer.

Une année de magie [a year of magic]

By virtue of my success in fine arts, my sculpture professor, Mr. Rosenberg, said he wanted me to work a little longer and a little harder. He knew I would benefit from a more intensive fine arts and interior design course of study. Mother and I discussed opportunities, costs and realities. After considerable deliberation and my landing a partial scholarship, based upon recommendations from Mr. Rosenberg, I was able to attend Fontainebleau, a medieval chateau outside of Paris, France, to study at the Chateau Écoles des Beaux Arts et Musique. I flew overseas to delve even deeper into my field of fine arts and interior design. My graduate school university was built in 1528 by King Francis 1 and was officially founded in 1648. In 1923, it was recognized as one of the UNESCO (The United Nations Educational, Scientific and Cultural Organization) top heritage sites.

Château de Fontainebleau, France

The excitement of studying in this historic structure was exploring its five *etages* (levels). The first floor was designated for sculpture, the second for painting, the third for architecture, the fourth for a particular kind of rendering, and finally, the fifth floor, set aside for live modeling. I loved every single one of the classes I took, all of which were taught in French.

I was there only for a year, but the time was magical. Charles de Gaulle (1890–1970) was president of France, and NATO headquarters was located in the town of Fontainebleau. Upon arrival, I excitedly took my luggage up to my room in the hotel dormitory directly across from Fontainebleau and met my roommate, Ruthie. She was French-Canadian and hailed from McGill University in Montreal, Quebec,

Canada. We clicked immediately. She took one look at my name tag and declared, "I cannot call you this 'Grass Gan' (her pronunciation of Grace Guin). No, no. I will call you Gigi (pronounced *Gee Gee*)."

So that's how I got my moniker at the age of 22. I embrace that name to this day. Ruthie was studying in the school of music, under the famous teacher, pianist, conductor and composer Nadia Boulanger (1887–1979). Ruthie was and still is a magnificent pianist and a long-time personal friend.

During our free time, Ruthie and I met and conversed with so many uniformed military men stationed at NATO Headquarters in Fontainebleau – young French, English, Canadian, Belgian and German officers. I took a liking to a young German by the name of Lutz Schultze Von Ronhoff, III. Everybody called him "Schultzie." He was 6'2", blond and drop dead gorgeous. Since Schultzie was blond, I decided to buy some peroxide, poured it all over my hair and magically transformed from brunette to blonde. While I was still at Fontainebleau, Ruthie used my trusty Polaroid instant camera to snap a picture of me standing next to Schultzie in his formal uniform. I proudly sent it back to Mother in Washington, D.C. Her reaction made me think we were on the verge of World War III.

Mère is very angry!

Mother wrote me because she couldn't reach me by phone. My roommate and I were rarely in the dorm. We were either in class at the Chateau, or we were down at NATO Headquarters eating, drinking and schmoozing (but not smoking) with the officers. Mother persisted with the calls and eventually got through to my roommate. I was out. When I returned, Ruthie told me, "*Oh, Mon Dieu! Gigi*! You must call your *mère* right away. She is very angry."

"Uh oh," I thought, assuming Mother was upset because I bleached my hair. It turned out her call had nothing to do with the color of my crowning glory. Mother had seen that picture of me standing with a German officer and she absolutely lost it. She laid me out in lavender saying, "You will never, ever see that German officer again, or there will be no further tuition at Fontainebleau, *COMPRENDS?*"

Keep in mind, I was a "Baby Boomer," born after World War II. I read about the war in my history books, but it did not have such profound significance to me as it did to Mother. How dare I go out with a German officer? She remembered how close we came to losing the war. That subject was never brought up again, but my photo with Schultzie stuck in her craw for the rest of her life.

From that point on, Schultzie was out of my life. But I dated a darling young Canadian Mounted Policeman and a few American and British officers. Nothing serious – just a lot of fun. I was always a proper young lady and kept my virginity. I did, indeed… although sometimes, it was challenging.

"Chopsticks" duet with the maestro

Earlier, while I was still at William and Mary, Mother became very well-known and respected in Washington, D.C. as a formidable forensic pathologist. But all work and no play makes for a dull lady, and Mother balanced her long professional hours indulging her passion for classical music. She was a regular at the Kennedy Center for the Performing Arts and was a familiar face at post-concert receptions. There, she came to be good compadres with none other than the world famous violinist Jascha Heifetz (1901-1987). Her medical reputation preceded her. She, in turn, admired his masterful musicianship. One night, they were chatting and Mother mentioned that her daughter was in graduate school in Fontainebleau.

"Fontainebleau?" Heifetz exclaimed. "You mean the French School of Fine Arts and Music?"

"Yes, that's exactly what I mean," Mother responded, matter-of-factly. "Right outside Paris. Why?"

"At the end of summer, my close friend, Arthur Rubinstein, is going there to perform a very special concert," Heifetz replied. After that conversation, Heifetz wrote to Maestro Rubinstein to introduce me: "Maestro, I have a dear doctor friend whose daughter is studying at Fontainebleau. It would be a thrill for her if you would meet her."

My Fontainebleau alma mater has rich history. Built in the Middle Ages as a fortress, it later served as a palace of privacy for royalty, as French kings would bring their paramours to Fontainebleau to escape the Parisian heat and humidity of Versailles. The Jeu de Paume (English translation: *the Playing of Games* – renamed the *Galerie Nationale de l'Image* in 1991) was constructed in the 17th Century as the world's largest indoor tennis court. It was eventually turned into the world's most spacious game room. Here was the symphony hall where, later that summer, Rubinstein was to make his grand appearance performing Chopin.

Because of my mother's request and Heifetz's crucial letter of introduction, before that concert, I met Maestro Rubinstein. He couldn't have been more gracious. I played Debussy's "Clair De Lune" for Rubinstein, and he asked if I could perform anything else. Having had six years of piano lessons decades earlier, I jokingly admitted that the only other piece I was comfortable playing was "Chopsticks."

With that, Maestro sat down with me on the piano bench and to my great honor, we played "Chopsticks" together.

Pianist Artur Rubinstein in 1968

CHAPTER 7

Je Suis "Gigi"

My 12 months in Fontainebleau comprised one of my most exciting years. But all good things seem to have a timeline, and with my studies completed, it was time for me to bid France a fond *adieu* and board an Air France plane back to the States. As we ascended, I gazed longingly out the window, watching the sites and people I had come to embrace as my own get smaller and smaller until they seemed to disappear in the mist. It was bittersweet. I marveled at my extraordinary experiences and was sad to leave. On the other hand, I was going home a new woman. I had evolved from Grace to *Gigi*. I couldn't wait to share my new moniker with my mother.

When she met me at Washington National Airport (now called Reagan National Airport), she raced over, threw her arms around me and exclaimed, "Oh, Grace, I am absolutely thrilled to see you again! Sweetheart, I missed you so much."

"Oh Maman!" I corrected her. *"Ce n'est pas Grace – Je suis Gigi!"* Mother looked at me and flatly replied, "What the hell are you talking about?" Mother never cussed, so I knew she meant business. "We've got generations of Graces in our family – my grandmother and mother, me and now you. You're not gonna be Gigi." Undaunted, I refused to respond when she called me "Grace." From that moment on, Mom finally acquiesced, but being such a steel magnolia, it took quite some time.

Once I got back to Arlington, I was already planning another new chapter and revved up for the next stage of my education and development. I had been awarded a partial scholarship to the New York School of Interior Design because my Fontainebleau interior design professors recommended me. Further, Mother instinctively realized that I needed to learn what the top fashion and interior designers were creating in New York.

A stranger is a friend I haven't met yet

Still actively protecting my honor, Mother arranged housing for me in what I called a nunnery – the Barbizon Hotel for Women, located smack in the middle of uptown Manhattan, at 63rd and Lexington Avenue. This hotel didn't allow men above the first floor, so Mom rested easier knowing I wouldn't be entertaining male guests.

What a thrill studying at the New York School of Design in midtown Manhattan. The curriculum included every imaginable interior design and space-planning concept, architectural schematic, furniture design and what the most renowned interior decorators were creating for their clients. It was a total immersion school for *de la derrière mode* (of the latest fashion).

One day, on a fairly long break between classes, I walked into a Horn & Hardart Automat. It was an affordable cafeteria where I could sit at the counter by myself and nobody would bother me. Who should walk in and sit on the stool next to me but a handsome gentleman? He looked as if he was as hungry as I was. Since "a stranger is a friend I haven't met yet," (one of Mother's sayings) we started chatting. Anthony was his name. He was from Palermo, an exotic city on the island Sicily, Italy.

We gobbled our sandwiches, chatting easily before we realized that an hour had flown by. If I didn't leave that minute, I'd be late for my next class. Rather than part company, he opted to walk me to school and hesitantly asked me out on a date. He looked fairly safe. Besides, I knew that my virginity wasn't in danger with him. After all, I was living in a nunnery! I said yes.

We saw each other about once a week for several months. Then, one weekend, he asked me out on his yacht. I had never been on a private boat of any kind, much less a yacht, so I agreed. Anthony picked me up and drove me to East River Basin, where his yacht was anchored. There were several other young ladies present, escorted by good looking young men.

We got underway and were enjoying snacks and fine Italian wine when all of a sudden, a deafening airhorn burst our revelry. We heard another blast as a boat came up behind us. It was the New York Coast Guard and they were closing in fast.

We ladies were bewildered as we observed the quick reactions of the men on board. Out of their pockets and from under lifejacket bins, our dates started frantically throwing weapons overboard. Surprise! They were part of the Italian Mafia. As exciting as that evening had been, this was the last date I had with Anthony. I imagine that if I mentioned the event to Mother, she would have been just as angry as she was seeing the Polaroid picture of Schultzie and me. I had to say goodbye to Tony, just as I had done to the German officer a year earlier.

From that point on, I decided to investigate my dating pool a little more carefully.

Big Apple, here I am

As a student at the New York School of Interior Design, possessing the unbridled confidence of youth, I was determined to master the world of art, architecture, furniture and interior design. That was a lofty goal, because as I later learned, a person can spend a lifetime amidst these fine arts and never truly master them. In any case, I poured myself into my studies. I also

endeavored to "pay it forward," as Mother taught me. One fine day, I set out from the Barbizon Hotel for Women and walked 15 minutes to Memorial Sloan Kettering Cancer Center, where Mother had been a physician when I was very young. I registered to be a "Candy Striper." I didn't know exactly what that job entailed, but I'd heard Mother speak highly of hospital volunteers who pushed carts to offer newspapers, magazines, treats, candies, lotions and other items patients might want.

They outfitted me in a cute little pink and white striped apron and cap. For the following two years, every Tuesday and Thursday after my design classes, I did what I could to comfort sick and frightened pediatric patients. I wasn't a doctor, but just being in the same environment where Mother aided and nurtured the lives of so many children, I felt a powerful connection with her. As a Candy Striper, in my own humble way, I followed in the footsteps of the phenomenal physician who had raised me. Each time I pushed my cart from room to room on the pediatric ward, I felt Mother's arms wrap around me. It gave me an overwhelming sense of comfort and security. I was as close as possible to Mom without actually being a doctor.

If you can make it here, you can make it anywhere

While at the Barbizon Hotel, I met a delightful young gal. She was one of the several talented up and coming actresses who lived at the Barbizon Hotel and came to the Big City to study acting. This particular aspiring actress happened to have the sweetest southern accent. She lived across the hall from me and we got to know each other. We had much in common. She was also born in Birmingham, Alabama. She asked where I had gone to school and I told her the College of William and Mary. I then learned she graduated from Birmingham Southern College – the same institution Mother attended decades earlier. We went to lunch several times, and she confided in me that she was bound and determined – typical of a southern steel magnolia – to stay in Manhattan until she made a name for herself.

This lovely young woman became a successful actress and appeared in quite a few plays and television shows. Soon after I left New York, she became the actress who played Sabrina in the 1970s television series, *Charlie's Angels* and Mrs. King in the 1980s' *Scarecrow and Mrs. King.* Her name is Kate Jackson, another super steel magnolia.

Those two exciting years in New York City flew by in a heartbeat. Studying hard, having friends like Kate Jackson, enjoying my work as a Candy Striper – all these memorable experiences laid a solid foundation for my interior design profession and adult life. But I was champing at the bit to put my education into action.

CHAPTER 8

Spreading My Wings

As exciting as life was in New York City, there was so much I missed in the nation's capital, like our wonderful home on Abington Street. So, I decided to come back to Arlington and was thinking about renting my own apartment. Mother, however, had other ideas. She pleaded, "I have an empty bedroom upstairs, Darlin'. It used to be yours. I would just love to have you under my roof again." Besides, even though I would be earning an income, I realized life at Mom's would be more economical.

I landed a wonderful job at Executive Interiors, a design studio in downtown Washington, D.C. I was assigned both residential and commercial clients, helping them identify and fulfill their design dreams. At last, I was able to pay Mom back a little for all she had done for me. With my very first paycheck, I gave her rent money, which she reluctantly accepted.

My familiarity with Washington, D.C., helped me get to know many professionals who wanted their offices upgraded. My world centered around corporate design, which meant offices, conference rooms and reception areas requiring legal-sized files, executive posture chairs, huge conference tables, spacious desks and matching credenzas. My first assignment was designing office spaces for American Airlines' corporate headquarters. This challenging opportunity served as a tremendous learning experience that lasted about a year. Thanks to my intensive studies and the tricks of the trade I'd learned from the marvelous community of New York interior designers, Executive Interiors knew I was qualified.

While I was totally absorbed with layout details of office interiors, in walked a fellow named Raymond Schiff.

"I just closed my New York City real estate business and want to get established in the District of Columbia," the man explained. "I've leased space in northwest Washington, D.C., and hope you can design the interiors."

"Certainly," I replied, taking out a fresh legal pad to jot down his specifications. "Let's get started." And start we did. Over the following four months, I designed and furnished an efficient and professional conference room, the executive offices and a comfortable reception area for Raymond's First Met Realty Corporation. While we were still working together, Raymond said he wanted to take me out. I told him that I never mixed business and pleasure. However, I did indicate that after his offices were completed to his satisfaction, we might get together.

Once Ray paid the final invoice, I mentioned to Mother that I was going to go out with this gentleman from New York – the Bronx. She said in her Southern drawl, "New York? Did you tell me he was from New York?" As a Southerner, Mother had a "thing" about Yankees. She wasn't too terribly happy when I started dating Raymond. He seemed different from the other men I had known at the College of William and Mary, or in France, and without a doubt, Mafioso Anthony.

He appeared to be very generous. In reality, he was on the prowl for a single lady with no baggage who made enough money to pay his ex-wife's alimony and child support. (Could I really have been that gullible?)

Ray appeared to be a total gentleman and very accommodating. He took me to dinner at some of the most toney restaurants in the Washington, D.C., area. Having grown up without a father, I really didn't know what it was like to get that much time and attention from a man. Daddy had walked out of my life when I was two, so I was pretty careful with my heart. I tended to like older gentlemen, perhaps because they reminded me of the father I never had. Raymond was eight years my senior.

About 18 months into our growing relationship, Raymond took me to an upscale restaurant called Sans Souci, which is French for "Without Care, Without Worry." It was a place the rich and famous frequented. At the table left of ours sat Senator Daniel Patrick Moynahan. Al Capp, the American cartoonist who created the *Li'l Abner* comic strip, was seated at the table to our right. As Raymond pulled out my chair, he placed a small Gucci gift box in front me. The card on the box said, "I just want to put a little chain around you."

When I was a graduate student in New York, every once in a while, I window shopped at Bloomingdale's or Lord & Taylor. Only occasionally would I pop into Gucci's on Fifth Avenue. But I just looked. I never bought anything because their jewelry and accessories were entirely out of my price range. So, with great curiosity, I opened the box to find a stunning gold and diamond Gucci bracelet. It was the most beautiful bling I'd ever seen. From that moment on, I felt that this was a man above all men. I should probably marry him, I thought. Soon, in 1973, he proposed and I accepted.

Our wedding took place in Mother's home. However, almost immediately after we exchanged vows, Raymond inexplicably complained he wanted to return to Manhattan. He missed his life in the big city. None of his real estate negotiations in the District had worked out as he had planned.

Mother begged us to stay in Washington, D.C. She had missed me while I was attending the College of William and Mary and even more so when I was across the ocean in France. Now, she would be deeply saddened to see me leave again. But Raymond was my husband, and while I was torn, I put his needs before Mother's. We packed up and drove 230 miles to New York City, with our puppy and kitten in the back of Raymond's Cadillac Eldorado convertible. We moved into a resort complex called the River Edge Apartments, just north of Yonkers in Westchester County. We rented a luxurious suite overlooking the breathtaking Hudson River and New Jersey Palisades. Thanks to little Donald Wallace (from whom I had inherited the guppies) I have a passion for all things aquatic – oceans, rivers, lakes, ponds, even fountains. I was delighted with our unobstructed view of the Hudson from every room in our apartment. Because of my interior design portfolio, it wasn't long before I landed gainful employment at Furniture Resources, on the 10th floor of the Squibb Office Building, located then at 745 Fifth Avenue. It was directly across from the ritzy Plaza Hotel.

One floor below us were the architectural offices of Edward Durell Stone (1902-1978) the famous architect who, in 1971, designed the Kennedy Center for the Performing Arts in Washington, D.C. He had also designed luxury two-level apartments for celebrities in New York City. At that time, he was one of the most well-respected, sought-after architects in the world, and just think – his office was directly below mine.

My very shrewd boss, Mark Solomon, was able to get referrals for interior design projects for luxurious apartments from Edward Durell Stone's architectural offices. What a coup!

John & Yoko

To get to work, I took the Hudson River train down to Grand Central. I then walked up to my Furniture Resources office, looking at the exquisite shops and huge office buildings on both sides of Fifth Avenue. I enjoyed the expansive views of Central Park. I felt I had arrived, reveling in my good fortune at being able to work in this firm. I was given some well-known clients, the first of whom were John Lennon and Yoko Ono. After the Beatles had broken up, John and Yoko had lived in hotels on Fifth Avenue, but were uncomfortable with the never-ending attention John's celebrity status drew. In 1973, they moved to a gothic cooperative on 77th and Central Park West called The Dakota. There they stayed, in apartment 46, until John was murdered in December, 1980.

John and Yoko were my clients from 1973 to 1975. Never in my life have I worked with people as caring and as interested in the design process as those two. They were very spiritual and had a relaxing ease about them. John loved looking at the improvements and refurbishments with the innocence of the little boy from Liverpool. He loved the relative anonymity the Dakota offered, at least initially. After John's death, it seemed everybody discovered where the couple had lived. The Dakota has been home to quite a few musicians, artisans and literary geniuses for decades. Yoko Ono still lives there.

Where John was laid back, Yoko was quite a bit more challenging, but she always remained gracious. She had a totally eclectic sense of style. She admired a variety of designs from a broad range of furniture styles, hanging chandeliers and assorted wall coverings, all of which featured a comfortable Asian influence. I especially remember one afternoon when I brought in a dramatic Coromandel paneled black and gold lacquered eastern Indian screen, inlaid with ivory and a variety of shells. Yoko loved it – and treated that screen as a treasured luxury. I realized that pleasing them was one of my most successful design projects, and John and Yoko were among the most charming and accessible couples I had the honor of working with. There were others, though, who weren't so nice.

CHAPTER 9

The Defiant Client

After helping furnish John and Yoko's Dakota apartment, I was introduced to several other celebrity clients. But the one that stood out most was a former model whose name I will not divulge. Married to a well-known television personality, she required assistance furnishing their opulent Park Avenue penthouse overlooking Central Park. This client knew exactly what she wanted and nothing less would do. Her requests were quite specific for the living room, dining room, parlor and bedrooms.

Her final requirements were to design the penthouse bar area. I showed her contemporary stool options consistent with her fashion desires – a combination of contemporary and classic. Next, I pulled out appropriate swatches of fabric to upholster all the bar stools. I offered her velvet, silk, leather and a variety of other luxurious coverings. Her reaction was cold and bold.

"These textures are not what I have in mind," this *femme fatale* responded. "There is only one covering that will do."

"No problem," I replied. "We have accounts all over the world and can locate fabric from anywhere on the globe. Just tell me what you want and we'll find it." I leaned in, clipboard in hand, ready to take detailed notes. Then she said, "Listen very carefully. I want baby elephant scrotum on my barstools."

I couldn't believe my ears. I paused a moment, needing to collect myself. No one had ever asked me to cover their barstools with baby elephant scrotum. So I looked her in the eye and with all the respect I could muster, repeated, "Baby elephant scrotum?"

"Yes," she replied with a smirk. "Baby elephant scrotum. It is all I'm interested in. It is the softest texture on the planet and I want my guests to experience this while they are relaxing with a drink at my bar. These exotic coverings will heighten their tactile experience. So, yes, this is exactly what I want and will settle for nothing else."

My next sentence came without pause, or forethought, for that matter. With indignance from my very core, I blurted, "Excuse me. Do you know how many baby elephants you'll have to slaughter in order to cover your five barstools, ma'am?" I did, in fact, call her "ma'am," hoping this respectful address would snap her out of her horrific request. It didn't.

Without blinking an eye, she said, "Yes, I understand. It doesn't really matter, does it? Just make sure you get the barstools covered. I think we're done here."

I took a deep breath, and at that moment, became the country's fiercest animal rights activist. I clutched my clipboard and pen and threw them into my black portfolio, zipped it up, and hissed with rage, "Yes, indeed. We are done here. You can get yourself another designer."

As I stormed out of her apartment, I heard her yell something indiscernible. I am sure she meant to be insulting, but no matter. I'd had my fill of her arrogance and vile demands. I took the elevator to the first floor and exited onto Park Avenue to stomp the several blocks back to Furniture Resources. As I entered the office, my boss was waiting for me at the elevator. Not the least bit surprised, I knew that when I walked out of the apartment of that defiant client who wanted the softest, the most luxurious, the rarest and the most outrageous of everything, that she would pick up her phone and call my boss the second her request was denied.

He said, "What in the hell have you just done? Do you realize how important this client is?" He couldn't wait for my explanation. He was livid. I replied, "In your office. Now." I spoke to him as if I were the boss, and he needed to listen to what had just transpired.

"Mark," I said, slamming the door behind us. "I'm not going to service anyone who feels it is appropriate to have dozens of male baby elephants slaughtered to cover her barstools with lifeless scrotums." The blood ran out of Mark's face. He looked as if he would faint. But after a moment's pause and drawing a deep breath, he looked at me with the sincerity of the ages and stated, "Congratulations, Gigi. We don't need clients like that."

I was so relieved and so proud that I was able to work for a man of such integrity as Mark Solomon.

CHAPTER 10

The Ultimate Aphrodisiac

After refusing the baby elephant scrotum-seeking client, my boss had a new view of me. He assigned me to bid on a variety of important corporate projects. Two of our bids were successful and we won the contract to redesign the headquarters of Simon and Schuster, the major publishing corporation located near Rockefeller Center. The second was to be part of the design team to upgrade Saks Fifth Avenue's Manhattan offices.

Another project that I enjoyed a great deal was designing the headquarters of the car company Fiat, an Italian acronym for *Fabbrica Italiana Automobile Tornino*, which loosely translates into the "Italian Manufacturing of Automobiles in Turin, Italy." Gianni Agnelli, the grandson of Fiat co-founder Giovanni Agnelli, assumed operation of the company in 1966, and in the mid-'70s, was the owner of Fiat when Furniture Resources was awarded their extensive design contract.

Agnelli moved his American headquarters to New York City's Seagram Building at 375 Park Avenue. When Furniture Resources won this project, we were given carte blanche. In 1969, Fiat had invested in Ferrari, and money was no object. Agnelli wanted magnificence. The furnishings were expensive, luxurious and incredibly impressive. I was thrilled beyond words to be able to facilitate and manage this challenging project.

While on this assignment, I was in the Seagram Building so often that I met Phillip Johnson, the world-renowned architect who designed the structure. He was famous for his home in New Canaan, Connecticut, an original architectural feat that he called his "Glass House." He later invited me to visit his internationally famous residence. What an honor!

Built between 1947 and 1949, the building was 50 feet long and 35 feet wide, comprised entirely of glass – no brick and mortar walls. It was an exceptional structure, and thanks to the National Trust for Historic Preservation, it still stands today. Philip Johnson lived in that house until he died in 2005 at the age of 98.

My next and most challenging of the interior design projects I encountered in my five years in New York was for Adnan Khashoggi, the billionaire arms dealer from Saudi Arabia. In 1972, Aristotle Onassis financed the construction of the Olympic Tower on 641 Fifth Avenue, a block away from St. Patrick's Cathedral. Khashoggi and Onassis were friends and the former decided he needed to have his American headquarters in New York City. Khashoggi assumed two entire floors in the Olympic Tower – five bedrooms, six bathrooms, a variety of different game rooms, a home theater, private bar areas, a private library and a swimming pool.

Notably, in the early 1980s, Khashoggi was confirmed as the wealthiest man on the planet. To help him fill his private library, his design firm in Zurich, Switzerland, directed several other designers and me to find as many first edition books as could possibly be obtained. We endeavored to accommodate his every expectation. I scoured hundreds of booksellers, bookstores, publishers and antique book dealers to procure as many first editions as I could lay my hands on. His very favorite first edition, which took me nearly a year to find, was *The Seven Pillars of Wisdom* about the life of Thomas Edward Lawrence, based on the Arab Revolt against the Ottoman Turks. This book became the blockbuster movie, *Lawrence of Arabia*.

I met Khashoggi only once, and frankly, he was not a very friendly man. In 1973, he flew to New York in his private jet to attend an urgent United Nations meeting. When he arrived at his Olympic Tower second story apartment following the official U.N. gathering, he barged into his library where I was arranging books. The man spoke very little English, but he wanted first-edition English language books lining his library to impress his universal guests. It reminded me of F. Scott Fitzgerald's main character in *The Great Gatsby*, who hardly ever read a book, but made sure he had first editions of everything. In any case, my guess is that there was some sort of altercation at the U.N., because when Khashoggi picked up a Napoleon Bonaparte manuscript that stated, "The ultimate aphrodisiac is power," he slammed the book down. I'd never heard that expression before, but I'll never forget it. And I never saw Khashoggi again.

This demanding design project was to be my last as an interior designer in New York City. Because I adored the city so much, why did I leave? Because of a violent encounter with Mother Nature.

CHAPTER 11

The Blizzard of the Century

It was February of 1977. My husband, Raymond, was still a real estate broker in New York City with offices in Manhattan and the Boroughs. I was loving my career at Furniture Resources and Raymond's business was going well. Our lives were seemingly perfect. We were making money faster than we could spend it. Our lifestyle was Gucci, my Jaguar, Ray's Cadillac and gold-plated keys. Charity wasn't ever on our radar. Within five years, I would change my ways and re-embrace the values my mother taught me about the importance of giving back. But for a short time, I was incredibly self-absorbed, enjoying a world I'd never known.

Dali, Diamond and Destiny dinner

I enjoyed several encounters with rich, famous and infamous people, not because I was so well-known, but because I was lucky. Life is all about timing, I discovered. For instance, I had a once-in-a-lifetime encounter with the flamboyant Spanish artist Salvador Dali. As it happened, I was in a celebratory mood after completing one of my Fifth Avenue design projects and decided to stroll down mid-town Madison Avenue. In doing so, I passed the wonderful restaurant named *L'Aiglon*, French for "Eaglet" or "Little Eagle." I slowed my steps when I spied a debonair gentleman in the *porte-cochère*, (courtyard) of this expensive eatery, sipping a cocktail. I immediately recognized his unique mustache, gigantic red hat and fashionably large black cape.

Remembering that "A stranger is a friend you haven't met yet," I had no hesitation about approaching him. "*Buen dia,*" I smiled at him. He looked up, a little surprised. Then I continued, "Mr. Dali, I want to thank you so much for your seductive masterpiece, *The Three Graces.*"

He sat back, removed his sunglasses and remarked, "Oh my dear, you have my painting, *The Three Graces?*" "Yes, sir, I certainly do," I replied. "I want you to know how very meaningful that painting is to my family.

You see, my grandmother is Grace Hawkins. Mother is Grace Hughes, and I am Grace Hawkins Guin. In my family, we are The Three Graces. Mother knew how much I loved your work, so she bought a lithograph of *The Three Graces*. You should know how your work has brought greater closeness to the relationship between my grandmother and mother, and more especially, between my dear mother and me. I love it, and I shall always cherish it."

He was pleased and invited me to sit down.

"Would you care to join me for a drink?" he inquired. Naturally, I accepted and we had a brief but lovely midday meal. It was a memorable hour, so much so that I even recall what I ordered – an almond brioche and a small cognac.

Another time, I had the thrill of seeing Neil Diamond up close and nearly personal. I am a huge Neil Diamond fan. My husband, Raymond, surprised me with front row seats for Diamond's *Hot August Night* concert in New York at Forest Lawn Tennis Stadium. For me, it couldn't get any better than that. Well, maybe with one exception. On

One of Salvador Dali's *The Three Graces*

our last night in New York City, Raymond took me to dinner at Windows on the World Restaurant on the 107th floor in the North Tower of the World Trade Center. The food was exquisite –the view, beyond the beyond. Before September 11, 2001, when a terrorist attack felled the famous Twin Towers, it had been called the world's most specular restaurant. And truly, it was.

It was a dark and stormy night

The catalyst for our move from New York to California was the unprecedented blizzard of February, 1977. Mother Nature played a cruel trick. More than five feet of snow had fallen in a matter of hours in New York City. I remember being at my desk and looking out the window at the accumulation on the streets 10 floors below. The snow showed no sign of stopping. My boss, Mark Solomon, came in and said, "You know, Gigi, I think you had better get the hell out of here…NOW!"

That day, I'd worn a pair of boots with heels and a light coat – nothing substantial enough to combat the icy drifts of snow covering the sidewalks. I packed up my briefcase and when I hit the ground floor, I saw that taxis, busses and private cars were paralyzed. Nobody was going anywhere, so I walked all the way down to Grand Central Station to catch the Hudson River train that would eventually take me back home to Westchester County. It took me almost two hours to walk some 20 long blocks from 59th and Fifth Avenue to Grand Central – freezing in my light outerwear.

I had no idea what was happening with the subway and trains, but I was about to find out. When I arrived at Grand Central, I asked a conductor when the next train would be leaving. He said, "None of the trains are moving. I have no idea how long it's going to be before they start running again."

It was 5 p.m. I waited until about 6:30. As darkness and even colder temperatures descended, an announcement blared over the public address system. The Westchester County train was delayed, but it would be coming in the next half hour. Finally, when the train arrived, it was standing room only, with no heat. Still, we chugged ahead. Then, somewhere between Manhattan and Westchester County, a tree, frozen with ice, fell across the train tracks, delaying us further.

The train was stopped dead in its tracks. It was now close to 9 p.m., and the passenger cars still had no heat. We had to wait. Consolidated Edison (Con Ed) engineers didn't arrive to remove the fallen tree until midnight. Standing for hours, we were crammed together in the freezing train. Just imagine what the restrooms were like!

That evening, two passengers suffered heart attacks and one was reported to have had a stroke. I will never forget that chilling ride as long as I live. I finally got home at 2:30 in the morning, where my husband was warm and cozy. Ray was smart enough to have left his office early, driven home, tucked his car in the garage and enjoyed a comfortable evening.

I, on the other hand, was uncomfortable, to say the least. There were no cell phones at the time, and I had no way to reach my husband. He was absolutely frantic when I finally pounded on the front door. I couldn't even grip the keys to put them in the keyhole, because some of my fingertips were frostbitten. When Ray opened the door, he put his arms around me, and I said, "I'm freezing! Get out of my way." I flung my briefcase on the couch and sat down, totally exhausted. The first words that came out of my mouth were, "Raymond, there has got to be a better way."

He looked at me and said as only this smug Bronx New York gentleman would say, "All right, Sweetheart, where would you like to move?"

Without hesitation, I said, "San Diego," and here's why. During my junior year at William and Mary, I had a wonderful roommate named Sharon. Her mother would drive us up to Annapolis every month to stay in the "drag houses" (where Naval Academy midshipmen could accommodate their dates) for a weekend of dances and parties. Sharon was pinned – beyond going steady, but not engaged – to a midshipman. She thought I might enjoy meeting one of his contemporaries, Robert.

The following year, after graduation, Robert had gotten my phone number from Mother, and called me while I was in France to say that he had received the most incredible assignment. He said he was stationed as a JG (junior grade officer) at Miramar Naval Air Station in San Diego, now called MCAS, the Marine Corps Air Station-San Diego. The last thing he said to me was, "Living in San Diego is like dying and going to heaven!"

I remembered this as I sat shivering in the middle of our living room. Raymond packed blankets around me to heat me up. My husband blankly looked at me and remarked, "I've never been to San Diego and neither have you."

"I know," I stammered, still chilled to the bone. Then I told him about dating a Naval Academy midshipman and his glowing impression of sunny San Diego.

"Raymond, tonight frightened the life out of me," I said. "I am tired of the cold weather and I've had it up to my earlobes with snow. Please. I want to leave." Raymond responded that he was an East Coast Boy and didn't really want to move to California. But he promised that if New York City ever thawed out and he was able to see the pavement again, he would fly out and take a look at America's Finest City.

Come spring, Ray and his real estate partner took a flight from JFK to San Diego's Lindbergh Field. They stayed three nights in the Holiday Inn overlooking the Embarcadero. Ray called me early on the third morning to report, "Oh my God, Gigi – this place is Heaven." It was April, 1977. By the end of May, he turned all of his real estate properties over to his partner and we relocated to San Diego. I'd given my resignation two months earlier to Mark Solomon at Furniture Resources, bid farewell to all my fellow interior designers and said good-bye to New York City.

Then we packed up, including our Pomeranian dog "Champagne" and our Balinese cat "Martini" and headed west.

Sea to shining sea

Since neither of us had ever travelled across the country by car, we decided to enjoy the scenery, stopping along the way to get to know our beautiful nation. We took an entire month exploring many villages, towns, cities and states, traveling from "sea to shining sea." We explored and learned as much history as we could, absorbing the beauty and grandeur of our magnificent country.

From the Continental Divide through the Black Hills of South Dakota, panning for gold and visiting the burial site of Wild Bill Hickok and on to Mount Rushmore, making sure to visit Yosemite, Yellowstone, hiking the Grand Canyon, riding horseback around the rim of Zion and Bryce National Parks, and studying petroglyphs in Utah. We arrived in San Francisco a month later, where the Golden Gate welcomed us to California, and Highway 101 escorted us the remaining miles to our new home in San Diego!

CHAPTER 12

Seaport Village Success to Topless Bar Tragedy

Upon our arrival in 1977, Raymond assumed there would be reciprocity between New York and California real estate brokers licensure. When he discovered there was no such thing, he was outraged and in a fit, asserted he didn't need to be in real estate anymore. He talked his good friend and insurance associate, Eddie, into flying out here from New York and together, they opened a liquor store. They thought that would be a bizarre new adventure.

Although they had no idea how to run a liquor store, that didn't stop them. They leased a shop on Catalina Boulevard in Point Loma. Ray was happy discovering a more easy-going lifestyle. He would come home and discuss the business of the day. I was playing lots of tennis because we had joined a swim and tennis club here in San Diego, and I was loving my life of freedom. I wanted to get to know our wonderful San Diego County, without having to work right away. Since Raymond claimed he was going to be our breadwinner, that was fine with me!

The liquor store was doing all right, aside from the three times they were held up at gunpoint. When he came home after the third robbery, I told Raymond that he'd been very lucky they had taken only money and not his life. He said he understood, but instead of selling the liquor store, he bought a Rottweiler, figuring a vicious dog on the premises would deter robbers. We found a beautiful little Rottweiler puppy from a breeder in Orange County, just north of San Diego. We took her to the beach, then brought her to the ranch-style home we had rented. She was our baby. Ray trained her, and he took her with him when he went to work at the liquor store. Unfortunately, she was about as vicious as a lamb. She preferred licking customers to death over biting anybody. Finally, Raymond gave up on the liquor business and looked for new ventures.

By January, 1979, groundbreaking for Seaport Village was underway here in San Diego. We were curious. When we walked around this tourist mecca, I was excited and, for a little while, Raymond was, too. With its bayside location, 60-plus shops and a flock of restaurants, it appeared to be a goldmine for investors. Raymond and I decided to lease three shops that would appeal to tourists. Our Seasick Giraffe was an upscale clothing store, Graphic Expressions sold paintings and graphic art from local artists, and San Diego Souvenirs provided greeting cards, ball caps, T-shirts, little bottles of sand and tiny shells that said "Take a piece of San Diego home with you."

Shortly after the grand opening of our stores, Ray got bored. He wanted to do something on his own – something more suited to his personality, he said. He got tired of standing behind a counter helping customers. Instead of working the shops in Seaport Village, Ray decided to open up a bar similar to Pacers, a strip club in downtown San Diego.

Unbeknownst to me, Ray found a bankrupt restaurant building in Point Loma and with his partner, Eddie, rented the space. They called it "Crazy Eddie's Booby Trap."

Raymond showed his true colors

The lessor of the building wanted the names of the investors for security. Bold as brass, Raymond included my name, and then forged my signature on the restaurant contract. Ray and Eddie managed this place for six months, and I heard nothing about it, other than it was a restaurant that made quite a bit of money. The first time I learned about the real nature of their establishment was when we received an alarming call at three in the morning from the San Diego Police. That's when I learned the shocking truth. My husband was running a strip joint. Welcome to my world of Dr. Jekyll and Mr. Hyde.

Ray and Eddie hired a young man to provide janitorial services. Every Friday and Saturday night, Ray would close at two a.m. and stash all the profits in a backroom safe. He'd return early Sunday to collect the money and felt safe, since he took our Rottweiler for protection.

Late one Saturday night, the janitor arrived after the bar was closed to clean up. He had learning disabilities, but was attending a local college in Point Loma. He was the only person there until the bar's sous chef and cook snuck in to break open the safe and steal the money. They forced the poor young man to his knees, gagged him and shot him, execution style, in the back of his head. Lying on the floor, he bled out in the kitchen where he had been mopping. Weeks later, police discovered the cook's car at Lindbergh Field, but the murderers – ex-cons – were never found.

Ray later told me that he was trying to be an "honorable gentleman" by hiring ex-cons because he believed everybody deserved a second chance. But city officials were not too thrilled that there was a topless bar in Point Loma where there had been a brutal murder. The Booby Trap was permanently closed by the City of San Diego.

Following that tragedy, we continued maintaining shops at Seaport Village. Ray, however, had changed. He was half-hearted in business and, as I later discovered, he had lost interest in me and in our marriage.

CHAPTER 13

The High Price of Happiness: Abandonment!

In the summer of 1978, I gave birth to a precious little boy, whom we named Randall Hawkins (the middle name a nod to my lineage) Schiff. Being a mother and feeling the joy and responsibility of parenthood generated my need to provide him with a wonderful life. What better place to raise a child than San Diego?

Seaport Village was officially opened and we were in charge of running our three shops. It was an enormous amount of work – managing the stores and caring for Randall. But it was so fulfilling. On my days off, I'd go swimming with my baby and my friends, and then haul myself back to Seaport Village early the next day. It was exhausting. It was also one of the best times of my life.

Amidst this flurry of activity, I became pregnant again. I should mention that going into the marriage, Raymond asserted he did not want us to have children. He explained that he had been married before, already had two children and sure as heck didn't want any more. But since we had Randall, he never voiced the same objections.

Because I was raised as a lonely only child, I didn't want Randall to grow up alone and was happy knowing my son would soon have a sibling. By virtue of being in San Diego, "America's Finest City," and also being a mom, playing tennis, going up to the club and watching my son grow up, I was living the dream. Life couldn't be any better. But I didn't know how bad it was going to get.

At the very end of June, 1981, I was ready to give birth to a second son, to be named Cameron Crockett (another nod to my lineage) Schiff. It was a long and painful delivery. I thought Raymond was going to be my Lamaze coach. He was supposed to show me how to hold my shoulders, to look at a very important focal point, and breathe hard to get over the labor pains. Those were the plans, anyway.

That's not the way it played out.

When my water broke after having played tennis early in the morning, I raced home and called Raymond. He was at one of our Seaport Village shops. I told him my condition and that my labor pains had begun. Raymond said he would be home soon.

Well, Raymond didn't come home. Five hours later, he still hadn't shown up. It was closing in on noon. I was now anxious because the labor pains had begun to come more frequently and more ferociously, and I really was not doing well. I knew I couldn't drive myself to the hospital. I needed him. I called the obstetrician and said my husband would be home promptly. I was really in a lot of pain and I knew I had to get to Kaiser Permanente Hospital ASAP!

My obstetrician said, "Call a taxi, Mrs. Schiff. You need to get here now."

"Well, my husband's at work over at Seaport Village," I assured the doctor, as well as myself. "I know he will be here shortly. And he will get me to the hospital quickly. Promise."

It was almost two p.m. before I saw Raymond. I was in distress. We had a great big comfy poof that the Rottweiler slept on – a big circle of foam filling. It was the only place I could be comfortable lying down. Ray sauntered in the door and said, "All right, let's go."

Leaving our home in Scripps Ranch, he didn't drive to the hospital. Instead, he went directly to Point Loma to the Sumitomo Bank building. He had a phone in the car way back in 1981, in his Cadillac Eldorado convertible. He called ahead, and a vice president and a loan officer were waiting outside the bank for us to drive up. The officer gave Raymond a bunch of papers and asked that we both sign them.

I was trying to stay on top of the labor pains, wondering why the hell we needed to stop at a bank in Point Loma. And why was I signing all kinds of papers? But I was in no condition to ask questions. Raymond said it was nothing important, that I should just go ahead and sign them.

I had no idea what I was signing. In my great pain and worry, I only remember scribbling my name. All I could think of was getting to the hospital to let this little creature come out. By the time we pulled in to the ER, it was three in the afternoon. Ray had already called the obstetrician, and there were two nurses standing at the door. They loaded me into a wheelchair and transferred me directly to labor and delivery. I was dilated to almost seven centimeters!

Things didn't look good. They wanted to hurry through this procedure, but my labor pains weren't continuing the way they were supposed to. At four p.m., Raymond announced he needed to go out for a breath of fresh air. I had no energy to stop him. I forced myself to keep looking at my focal point, which was a picture of my precious Randall.

I had no idea where my husband had gone. I was in pain and the contractions hurt like hell. But the baby was still not coming. I was going to be induced. I thought I knew pain, but never in my life had I felt such agony as when they started injecting me with Pitocin to help force the delivery of this baby.

Raymond was gone for over an hour. I didn't care about him. All I knew was excruciating pain and deep fear. It didn't look as if the baby would come. I was afraid that my son might not make it, and I wasn't sure that I would, either.

Then, in walks my husband. He was bright red. He looked horrible, sweating all over. I asked, "Are you all right?" He said he had gone out and walked around the hospital for a smoke. Several weeks later, when the bill arrived from Kaiser Permanente, I found out he had made an appointment to have a vasectomy that same afternoon while I was in labor. Thus the explanation for his bright red face covered in sweat.

Maybe it was something about Raymond's return and maybe the Pitocin was working, but finally my adorable little Cameron arrived. I had a hematoma and was bleeding profusely. I was absolutely exhausted, worried and very scared.

The obstetrician checked in to make sure Cameron was all right. He put the tiny baby on my chest and said, "We're going to cut the umbilical cord now and I'm gonna leave the two of you alone to bond with your little newborn. Don't worry about the bleeding. We'll take care of that later." Then the doctor left me alone with Cameron. And Raymond.

Raymond stood up, walked over to the bed, put his hand on the little blanket where Cameron was lying on my chest. He never looked at his son. With a deadened stare, he said to me, "I am leaving. I am leaving you, I am leaving California. I told you I never wanted kids. You went against my will. You not only had one, Randall, but now you have another."

His eyes remained trained on mine as he raged, "I can't stand it anymore. I don't want to be here any longer. I didn't want any children. I'm getting the hell out of California. I'm going to Europe to write. My spirit has been aligned with those of greatness, like Leonardo and Michelangelo."

I was holding Cameron. I got up on one elbow as the tears began streaming down my face. And I said, "What the hell are you smoking? Raymond, what are you talking about?"

"I hate California," he said. "I don't want to be a father again. I can't stand you. I'm leaving!"

With that, he walked out of the room. Months later, Raymond's mother told me that he had planned this all along, that he was seeing another woman, and there had been others. I also discovered that the quick trip to the bank meant Raymond could withdraw an extra $40,000 dollars taking out a second trust deed on our home. I had no idea that he was having affairs behind my back and that he had made plans in advance that once this child was born, he and his girlfriend would fly to France. In fact, she was waiting in the reception area on the third floor of the hospital with two tickets to Paris. Their plane left just hours later.

This man I had promised to love and honor for the rest of my life, whom I had trusted with my heart and, yes, my purse, had turned coat and changed colors. I had been abandoned by my husband. I was beyond devastated. Eventually, a nurse came in and, knowing nothing of the drama that had just unfolded, chirped happily, "You'll be able to leave the hospital in about eight hours after you recover." To which I responded flatly, "Yeah. Wonderful. How the hell do I get home?"

When they rolled me into recovery, I looked at the bassinet that I had earlier decorated with blue ribbons. That pulled me from my state of shock and I began to gather what was left of my dignity and strength. Kaiser Permanente let me use the phone to call one of my very dear friends. I whispered to her, "Raymond left me. Can you pick me up from the hospital?" As I sat, completely numb, in my friend's passenger seat, I turned to look at the back seat where my precious little Cameron was lying in the ribbon-covered bassinet. That's when the reality of my circumstances really hit home! I let myself give in to racking sobs and wondered if I would ever stop crying.

I thought I was living the dream, but instead, I had just endured one of the worst nightmares of my life.

Six months later, Raymond and I were divorced. *Nolo contendere.*

CHAPTER 14

My Incredibly Brilliant Mother

I was about six months pregnant with my second child when, on March 30th, 1981, a maniac tried to assassinate President Ronald Reagan as he left the Hilton Hotel in Washington, D.C. The president was rushed by ambulance to George Washington University Hospital.

By then, Mother's reputation as a forensic pathologist was well known and respected. She was on staff at Georgetown University and Walter Reed Hospitals, and the National Institute of Health. On this particular day, however, she was teaching senior medical students at the very place Reagan was taken after the attempted assassination.

President Reagan was rushed into the ER and Mother was called in as one of the pathologists to trace the trajectory of the would-be assassin's bullet. It had lodged under his left arm, broke or shattered a rib or two, and punctured his lung, causing internal bleeding. Mother's assessment determined that while serious, the wound was not life-threatening. Her key insights and prognosis of the President's chances of survival directed the medical attention he was given once he was sedated and placed into surgery. Before the anesthesia took effect, Reagan told the First Lady, "Sorry, Nancy. I forgot to duck."

New languages

In addition to Mother being a forensic pathologist, earlier on, when I was still at college, I received a phone call from her.

"I'm flying up to Armonk [New York] for a few months," she said, as if it were nothing that she would be away from Washington, D.C., for an extended time.

"Where is Armonk?" I queried. "And why in the world are you going there?"

"Well, Dear," she patiently explained. "You know the IBM Headquarters in Westchester County? I have now been tasked with the overwhelming job of setting up electron microscopy laboratories for pathologists working in Veterans Administration Hospitals around the country. You may not know that electron microscopy is the study of the magnification of tiny objects that brings them measurably closer to the eye for intense examination and scientific scrutiny."

I took a moment, trying to absorb all of this before responding with my most erudite, "Um, I see, Mom." I didn't really understand. But what else could I say? Mom went to Armonk in 1963. She spent three months there learning to speak the language of Fortran and COBOL, and for 15 years, traveled around the country establishing laboratories for pathologists working in more than 100 V.A. hospitals to teach them the importance of electron microscopy. Yep, that was my incredibly brilliant mother.

I remember her calling me from Armonk one time to say, "Well, they think I'm bright enough to figure out all these computer languages. In fact, we're learning more and more about less and less and pretty soon we'll know everything about nothing." And that was her indomitable sense of humor.

This was the brilliant, humorous and extraordinarily capable woman who would come to my rescue after I delivered my second son and was lost in complete hopelessness.

CHAPTER 15

Pity Party Princess

The several days after my baby was born were a blur. I tried to process the fact that my husband had deserted us – left me high and dry with my three-year-old son, Randall, and my newborn, Cameron. The world had turned completely upside down.

Before I went into labor, I had every intention of calling my mother afterwards to tell her about her new grandson. But Raymond's sudden departure left me totally devastated. I simply couldn't work up the courage to dial the phone. The shock of Raymond's betrayal left me immobilized. How in the world was I going to feed us and pay all the bills? How could I possibly work and raise two children at the same time? Calling Mom to say, "Guess what? I have a new little baby boy. Oh, and my husband walked out" wasn't in the equation at the time.

I tried desperately to nurse Cameron, but because of the traumatic birth process, my milk hadn't come in. Somehow, those first few days, I managed to feed the baby with formula sent home from the hospital and satisfy little Randall with the snacks I had on hand for him. Clearly, we were a family in crisis.

Fortunately, when Mother didn't hear from me, she called.

"Hi, Sweetheart! Wasn't your little one supposed to be born about now?" I glanced over at the calendar. It was already the first week of July. Cameron had been born the end of June. I broke down and told her everything. She was on the next plane to San Diego.

Mother arrived and I cried and cried and cried. She stocked the pantry and got formula for the baby. I cried. She made all the meals, changed diapers, bathed her grandsons, did the laundry and tried to get me to eat. I cried. I didn't care about anything. I just cried.

After she washed the dishes and put the boys down for the night, she'd come up to my bedroom and try to talk with me, but I wouldn't respond. I would just lie there and cry. Sometimes, I read my Bible, but the words meant nothing to me. I felt like a complete failure. I couldn't even nurse my baby. While the hematoma had stopped bleeding, I was still in no condition to work. What would I do with no income? My faith was shattered. I had no hope. To me, life was over. So you know what I did? I kept on sobbing.

Mother with grandson Cameron

Rose gardens

After 10 days of enduring my pity party, Mother sat at the edge of my bed and said, "Darlin', I have to say something to you. I know you're upset, and I know you're surprised that things have turned out the way they have." Then she took my hand, looked me straight in the eye and continued, "Nobody ever promised you a rose garden."

I drew a breath that was about to be a sob, but instead, choked out, "Whhhaat?"

"Nobody ever promised you a rose garden," she explained. "I sure never did. Now, I'm tired of your whining, 'What am I going to do?' So, Sweetheart, sit up, get up, get dressed. Your husband's gone and you have to get on with your life. If you don't get the hell out of this bed and start taking care of yourself, don't think that I am going to hang around here forever. I have work to do back in the District of Columbia. I raised you better than this. If you don't pull yourself together, then I feel very sorry for you. You're not the lady I thought you were."

At this point, I was still crying. How could my sweet mother, who loves me so much, talk to me like this? I was in the depths of despair. How could she rip my soul apart by saying those things? Of course, she was absolutely right, but I couldn't see it. I couldn't see the proverbial forest for all the trees. Given what I had just gone through, there seemed to be too many damned trees.

She waited until my weeping subsided and then she spoke.

"I will make you a one-time offer," she said. "If you want to feel sorry for yourself for the rest of your life, and you don't think you have it in you to get up, get dressed, become employed and get on with your life, then here's what you do. Sell this house. Get rid of the dog, get rid of the cat and pack up the kids. I will fly you back to Washington and move you into my home in Arlington.

"You can have Grandmother Hughes' room. Your two boys can have your bedroom. I'll stay in the master bedroom. And I will work my ass off and support you and your children until you – you poor, pathetic little creature – can begin to think about taking care of yourself and your sons."

I could not believe Mother was aiming these sharp words at me. I felt like a piece of garbage. But Mom, in her infinite wisdom, knew exactly what I needed to hear. She tore me apart. She ripped out my very heart and left nothing but this whimpering, sniveling little gal who couldn't possibly be a steel magnolia like her mother was. If she had kicked me in the stomach, it wouldn't have made a more painful impression. I didn't realize it at the time, but those were some of the most important words my mother ever spoke to me in my 36 years on the planet. That's what it took for me to realize exactly what I had to do.

Mother quietly left my room. The next morning, I rose early, showered and dressed, and drove Mother to the airport. I hugged her and thanked her profusely. Then I told myself in no uncertain terms, "All right, it's time for this lady to start living again."

Taking stock

I looked into my savings, and thank the good Lord, had a little money left. With a bit of help from Mom, that saw me through the first year in terms of covering the mortgage, groceries and the many bills. Along the way, I did receive an interesting invoice from Kaiser Permanente. I opened the envelope, figuring it was the bill for labor and delivery of Cameron. But the contents had nothing to do with that. Instead, it indicated a procedure for Raymond Schiff. While I was suffering through my 15th hour of hard labor, he told me he was going out for a smoke break. Instead, he took the elevator to the fifth floor of the hospital and had a vasectomy. He made sure that he would never have another child, regardless of the woman he might have ended up with.

I admit, when we married, neither of us wanted children. We were too busy with our careers and living a life of indulgence. But my biological clock kept ticking and I eventually changed my mind. Raymond didn't. My husband had a vasectomy and left me totally responsible to pay the $5,000 bill. The good news was, I also had my wonderful sons. And thanks to Mother shocking me into reality, it took a while, but I had rediscovered my faith, strength and dignity-my Southern roots.

I guess if my so-called father, Joel Guin, could walk out on Mom when I was barely a toddler, then why wouldn't my husband walk out on his wife and sons? I thought, "like father, like husband." Without my mother, I never would have survived. I busied myself with important details, like hiring an attorney to get a *nolo contendere* (no contest divorce. On top of that, there were the boys to care for. And expenses to pay, including medical bills, legal fees, the monthly mortgage and, adding insult to injury, Raymond's vasectomy. That was colossally unfair, but my lawyer advised me that if I didn't pay up, my credit would be ruined. Life is not always fair.

Through this terrifically challenging time of my life, my Bible was my first source of solace and strength. When the going got really tough, I turned to my Bible and the Old Testament "Proverbs." Six months after Raymond flew to France with his floozie, I joined the illustrious Torrey Pines Christian Church in La Jolla. Both my babies were baptized and dedicated at Torrey Pines.

With Mother's help, this horrendous experience strengthened my faith beyond my wildest dreams. I began to believe in The Almighty more than ever before, as well as reconnect with my steel magnolia roots.

CHAPTER 16

Glad Tidings

Glad tidings came our way the Christmas of 1981 and the years to follow. My sons were growing up happy and healthy, and the two live-in ladies I hired were wonderful guardians. I passed the California Real Estate exam the first time I took it and hung my license with Caldwell Banker. Also, I kept in touch with several William and Mary alumni, who had emigrated to the West Coast from Williamsburg, Virginia, decades earlier.

One very special lady living in La Jolla was Dr. Patricia Sell. She was responsible for introducing me to Torrey Pines Christian Church. I felt at home there immediately and transferred my membership from National City Christian Church in Washington, D.C. Both Pat Sell and I are still members today.

Another wonderful William and Mary alumnus, by the name of Captain Robin Reighley, is a good friend who has kept in touch with me. Robin and his wife also found America's Finest City as appealing as Raymond and I had found it when we arrived. Right before Christmas, Robin knew I needed some glad tidings following both my sons' health challenges (explained later). He and his wife invited me to his annual Christmas party at the San Diego Yacht Club. Robin was one of four syndicate owners of a custom-designed 38-foot, ultra-light displacement vessel named *Cracker Jack*.

Knowing that Raymond had abandoned us that year, Robin did not want me spending Christmas alone. What a wonderful gift, to be included in such a beautiful celebration.

The San Diego Yacht Club had been decorated to the hilt with yachting decorations throughout the club. Several trees had been decorated with sailboats and San Diego Yacht Club pennants and burgees. During our festive holiday dinner, Robin seated me next to a gentleman who seemed to be alone. His name was Harris Hartman, another *Cracker Jack* syndicate owner. I realized what Robin's matchmaking plans were.

Harris and I got along so well that we talked all through dinner, drinks and dancing. As the evening wound down, Harris walked me down to the dock where *Cracker Jack* was moored. What a beautiful, custom-designed sailboat! Harris then walked me to my car and asked for my phone number. I expected there might be exciting "glad tidings" in the future.

That relationship became everything I could have asked for. We dated for over three years and spent wonderful weekends sailing *Cracker Jack* around the bay, into the ocean and down to Coronado. We loved that sense of freedom sailing allows, gliding silently in the water with the wind at our backs. It was enjoying those carefree adventures which ultimately lead me to my passionate love for the ocean.

One special evening, Harris and I discovered that Dennis Connor, Commodore of the San Diego Yacht Club, was going to be the Challenger of the America's Cup with his winged keel *Stars and Stripes* catamaran. Not only did I want to get involved, but I was able to watch *Cracker Jack* spar with *Stars and Stripes* while Dennis and his crew prepared for the pinnacle of achievements in the world of sailing. This prestigious race is the oldest yachting trophy in America, dating back to 1851.

On April 27, 1987, all of San Diego was watching Dennis Connor and his lightning-fast crew beat the New York Yacht Club, which had proudly held the Cup for 132 years. We were all excited to be at the yacht club celebrating Dennis's victory. Harris even took a picture of Dennis and me joyfully drinking champagne out of the treasured trophy.

At the evening celebrations, Dennis got up to the microphone at the yacht club. As he began to speak, he stopped as the audience heard a few chords from a guitar being played at the top of the staircase. As we all turned our heads, we heard a familiar voice singing the words, "To sail on a dream on a crystal clear ocean, to ride on the crest of a wild raging storm." It was John Denver singing his song, "Calypso," to the crowd. It was a magical moment. Not only for Dennis Conner, but for all of us realizing what winning the America's Cup for San Diego meant.

After the festivities, Harris and I were escorted to the yacht club dining area. I saw a man whom I recognized. I wasn't really sure who he was at first, but when we walked over to his table, he introduced himself as Theodore Geisel. Harris and I were standing next to Dr. Seuss and his lovely wife, Audrey.

I held it together. I wanted to tell him that I read *Green Eggs and Ham* 348 times to my boys. But instead, I said, "Good evening, Dr. Seuss. How are you?"

Ted Geisel said, "We couldn't be any better, and we are so happy for Dennis Connor." He then said, "Would you like to sit down and join us for dinner?"

They were just regular people. Audrey did most of the talking, but when Ted interjected, his conversation centered on the importance of education and the scholastic development of the University of California, San Diego (UCSD) through the years.

I then shared with them my mother's perspective on education. "The only true liberation is education." Ted and Audrey smiled and said, "How right your mother was."

Our conversation that evening centered on expanding the minds of children and was one of the most memorable dialogues I've ever had. Because of Ted and Audrey's passion and philanthropic generosity to UCSD, I made a promise to join them by furthering their commitment, ultimately resulting in both of my boys attending UCSD years later. Randall attended the Warren School of Science and Engineering – Cameron, the John Muir School of Economics. I know Dr. Seuss would be proud.

Having a partner for the years that Harris and I were together gave my life special significance. I had hoped that we could make the relationship permanent. Harris, however, had grown sons of his own and told me he really didn't want to be tied down in another relationship with young sons. Once again, it was time for me to reprioritize my life. I had to focus on my sons and my real estate career.

CHAPTER 17

It's a God Thing

My boys needed their mother. Further, I had a career to pursue and dreams to fulfill. I hired two lovely young women as child care assistants while I studied for my California real estate license. Because they were so caring and competent, I soon hired them as full-time live-in helpers. As luck would have it, the decision to hire helpers was just in the nick of time. My older son, Randall, was outside playing on a backyard rope swing when he fell off and landed face down in a pile of twigs, leaves and sticks. One of the sticks punctured his cheek less than a quarter inch from his left eye.

Head wounds are notoriously bloody and Randall came running into the house, covered in red. I threw a towel around his head and told the live-ins to watch Cameron, who was napping in his crib. While the helpers stayed with my baby, I raced to the Children's Hospital (now called Rady Children's Hospital) ER with Randall. Fortunately, they saw us immediately.

Randall was so scared at the sight of all that blood pouring down his face that he kept crying hysterically. Eventually, the bleeding stopped, but not the swelling. We were asked to stay at the hospital for eight hours until the pediatrician on duty assessed the damage. Randall's cheek required 25 stitches. The good news was that there would be very little scarring and his eye would be fine. Without live-in help taking care of baby Cameron, I don't know how I would have managed Randall.

I was not prepared for the next crisis. Shortly after Randall's accident, I heard Cameron crying in his crib early one Monday morning. I ran into the nursery and picked up my six-month-old baby. Cameron was burning up with fever and his body was bright red. Frightened beyond words, I called my pediatrician, Dr. Michael Sexton, immediately. He told me to meet him at his office as soon as possible. Again, thank heaven the live-in ladies were on hand so they could take care of Randall, who was still sleeping.

Despite the chill of a California winter morning, Cameron's fever raged. I bundled him up and we drove to Dr. Sexton's office. It was shortly before Christmas and Cameron had caught a cold. Apparently, overnight, his cough and cold had turned into a bacterial infection. My baby's young immune system couldn't handle the inflammation in his body. His colon had suddenly ruptured overnight and fecal matter was backing up into his intestines. Dr. Sexton diagnosed Cameron's condition as a fistula — not serious in an older person, but in an infant, it was life-threatening. He told me that without surgical intervention, my son had less than 12 hours to live. He made arrangements with the pediatric surgeons on duty at Children's Hospital. I raced there with Cameron and I turned him over to the pediatric nurse. Fortunately, that compassionate individual was a very good friend of mine, Betty Spangler – an elder at Torrey Pines Christian Church where I'd had Cameron dedicated the week before.

There is a Christian expression, "It's a God thing." Seeing Betty at the door of the pediatric surgery ward, my faith that my baby might survive increased.

I sat down on a cold, hard chair in the waiting room and prayed to The Almighty like I had never prayed before. I also called my minister, Dr. Clair Berry, and his wife, Charlotte, to request their prayers. They, in turn, contacted my entire Sunday Bible study classmates to engage them in prayer. Within the hour, Clair and Charlotte arrived at Children's Hospital to wait and pray with me.

After several anxious hours, the doctor sent us to a recovery room on the second floor, furnished with a crib and chairs, to await word about Cameron. Clair and Charlotte never left my side. They placed their Bible on the pillow of the empty crib and, several hours later, most of my Bible study classmates arrived to join Clair, Charlotte, and this emotionally drained lady, in intense prayer. We held hands, encircled the crib and called on The Almighty. That cold December Monday in 1981 seemed to last forever. But with so many caring couples providing support, my faith was bolstered. The very moment my minister's Bible was placed on that pillow in the empty crib, I knew I would see my precious Cameron again.

By early afternoon, I held my wriggly, squirming bundle of joy in my arms, even though he had tubes coming out of every orifice. Although he was far too young to remember that terrifying episode, Cameron endured residual pain as a toddler, and years later, loved the retelling of his remarkable recovery.

Cameron is a grown man with little ones of his own now, but to this very day, he still refers to that episode as having "a bomb in his butt."

CHAPTER 18

Breast Cancer and Cool Moss

Recently, a close girlfriend and I enjoyed dinner at one of my favorite local restaurants, Sammy's Woodfired Pizza & Grill. We sat outside, warmed by an outdoor fire pit. The embers drew my attention and out of the blue, I began to cry.

"Gigi," my dinner partner inquired with a mixture of concern and tenderness peculiar to women who have known each other a long, long time. "What's the matter?"

"Oh, writing my biography has dredged up so many memories," I replied, tears streaming down my cheeks. "Some good, some very bad. This fire triggered the recollection of a very difficult phase of my life."

"Would talking about it help?" she gently pressed.

"Maybe," I said, wiping my eyes. "I was remembering my experiences with breast cancer."

"I see," she said. "I am also a breast cancer survivor, Gigi. It's a horrible thing to go through. The good news is that we each survived this assault on our bodies. Could you tell me more?" I proceeded to relate the tale of my frightening struggle with cancer. Perhaps even more so, because breast cancer attacked me in my late 30s, when my boys were little. In addition to enduring the disease and treatment, the worry about what would happen to my children if I died was nearly paralyzing.

Back then, Mom suggested I start getting mammograms before I turned 40. Given her medical expertise and cancer research background, I heeded her advice. Even though I had no symptoms, I scheduled my first appointment when I was 37, the year after Cameron was born. The results came back fine. But when I had my second mammogram at age 38, a tumor had reared its ugly head. Again, I had no symptoms and could feel no lump. But my doctor told me that if the tumor had been allowed to grow until I could feel it, it would have been too late. I would have died shortly after discovering the tumor.

The diagnosis was deadly tubular mammary introductal adenocarcinoma. Treatment would be aggressive. Thank God I had listened to Mother. Early detection was my salvation. Also critical to survival was my mental state. For the sake of my young sons, I had to be strong to overcome this monster that had invaded my body. Yet I didn't feel strong. I felt vulnerable and afraid. I was no longer in control.

Fire walker

It was an incredibly stressful time. My husband had left me two years earlier and I was on my own – emotionally and financially – to provide for my precious sons. With job demands and making sure my babies were well loved and cared for, I had to be "on" 24-7. I was already on a steady diet of worry, but the diagnosis pushed me to the edge. Fortunately, I heard that self-help guru Tony Robbins was holding a *Mind Over Matter Firewalk Conference* at the Anaheim Hilton. I didn't know a lot about Robbins at the time, but I knew I had to create an arsenal of weapons to combat the cancer and fortify my courage. Hoping he could help me, I signed up.

Randall and Cameron were five and two at the time, so I arranged for my live-in ladies to stay with them while I handed my confidence and complete trust over to Tony Robbins for three days.

The intensive class started with 75 people. By the end of the weekend, fewer than half remained. I was among those who stuck around for the infamous "Firewalk." Throughout the conference, "You can do anything if you believe you can" was drilled into us. Our mantra was "Cool Moss," which we were instructed to say hundreds of times each day and as we fell asleep at night. I embraced this mantra and got in line for the walk. While it was touted as walking on fire, there were no flames. Yet the sight of 50 feet of red hot burning coals looming before me was plenty daunting. When it was my turn, summoning the mantra, "COOL MOSS," I gingerly stepped onto the coal bed and steadily made my way to the other end. I did it. No burns. Not a single blister!

When I completed the 50-foot grill, I realized I could fearlessly overcome cancer. It wouldn't be easy. Despite aggressive treatments with all kinds of nasty side effects, malignant tumors returned. Twice. Both times, I won the battle. But each occurrence left its mark on my body and spirit. The first time, the surgeon removed two-thirds of my left breast and inserted a drain that oozed for what seemed an eternity. When the drains came out, I had a careful look at my once beautiful and now marred chest. Emotion overtook me. It was a long time before I could view my breast without anguish, but eventually, thank God, I came to embrace the new me. In fact, I encourage all women who experience any level of mastectomy to accept the beauty of their alterations. Remember, those scars represent a hard-fought battle where you emerged victorious. We are not just survivors — we are THRIVERS.

A year later, another wicked tumor appeared. This time, it was a lobular carcinoma in situ and presented over my heart. Mother asserted that I should submit to radiation. For the first time ever, I refused Mom's medical opinion.

"Mother, I realize I am not a doctor," I countered, "But this is my life and my body and I absolutely refuse to let radiation come anywhere near my heart." Instead, I had surgery to remove the tumor and everything was taken care of. For the time being, anyway.

"Darlin', you were right," my mother admitted years later. "Radiation might have damaged your heart and possibly ended your life."

Eighteen years passed before the monster within reappeared a third time, attacking my right breast. My third operation was to remove the tumor. I went under the scalpel a fourth and fifth time to prevent potential spread to my lymph nodes. Then, I allowed radiation treatments, which seriously scarred my right lung.

I was older then, and had embraced humor as a survival tool. If you've had radiation, you know it burns like the devil. So I'd go in for each treatment wearing a bathing suit, beach hat and sunglasses and tell the techs, "I'm ready for my fun in the sun." They'd laugh. I kept them in stitches with blonde jokes. They loved my humor. I, in turn, desperately **needed** my humor to get me through the 40 radiation treatments. I took my strength from *The Man of la Mancha* theme song, "The Impossible Dream," and had every surgeon listen to the lyrics, knowing I had to beat breast cancer because I had two beloved sons who needed their mother. It was critical for me to be as strong as *The Man of la Mancha* so breast cancer would never take control of my life.

There would be other serious challenges in my future, such as bacterial and viral meningitis, not to mention a fatal car accident. But that's another chapter.

Time capsule

In 1992, Cameron wrote the following essay, which won top honors at the La Jolla Cancer Research Foundation, to be placed in a time capsule, scheduled to be opened in 2092:

Cameron Schiff

I know I am just a little kid, and you probably think I don't know much about cancer, but you're wrong. I do because my mom had breast cancer and she almost died. You probably don't care what happens to my mom because you have too many other things to do, but I do care about my mom and anyone else who has cancer, and I hope that there is a cure for almost every cancer in the year 2000. I hope you feel the same because if we try hard enough, by the year 2000 I am sure that we will have more cures than we have now. Besides it would be good if you found those cures because if you saved a rich person's life then they will probably give you alot of money. So look at it this way, you will be a hero and no doubt about it you will be rich.

So when you're working think of what I said and you will work alot faster, I promise.

CHAPTER 19

One of the Best Decisions I've Ever Made

After Raymond deserted us, life settled into a semi-routine for our little family of three. We called ourselves "The Three Musketeers." My boys grew steadily and really enjoyed school. I focused on them and my career. I had time in the evenings to help them with their homework, have dinner with them and read bedtime stories. Of course, they especially loved Dr. Seuss.

Despite a demanding work schedule, I volunteered one morning every week in each of my sons' classrooms, tutoring children in math, spelling and science projects. Both boys looked forward to having access to me during their school day. They were proud to have their mom help their classmates, too.

The Three Musketeers

The live-in ladies were a godsend, taking charge of Randall and Cameron after school until I got home from work. On weekends, whenever I wasn't holding open houses, I attended my boys' soccer matches, baseball games and tennis tournaments. Every weekday, after dropping my kids off at school, I concentrated on becoming the best real estate agent I could possibly be. My broker kept reminding me, "Real estate is not a 9-to-5 job. It becomes your life. You don't just try real estate. It tries you."

Try me, it did. There were residential caravans, houses to preview, meetings with potential buyers and open houses. It was a great way to discover the fascinating geography of San Diego. All of my time and effort paid off when Partners' Real Estate franchise awarded me Real Estate Agent of the Year in 1988. I accomplished this while raising my two boys as a single parent. In the process of working my backside off to keep body and soul together, a roof over our heads and occasional food on the table, I tried to keep a sense of humor. When money was especially tight and my boys would complain, "Mommy, I'm hungry," I'd look at them, smile and joke,

"Didn't I feed you yesterday?" You don't make it through life unless you have an off-the-wall, wacko, bat-shit crazy sense of humor. And the kids would giggle, "Mom, stop. That's not funny!"

"Okay, okay," I'd respond with high drama. "I'll make you some dinner."

A tall, distinguished gentleman

Several years into my wonderful real estate world, I held a Sunday open house in Scripps Ranch, when in walked a tall, distinguished gentleman escorting a young couple. I greeted him with, "Good Afternoon. Welcome, and would you be kind enough to sign the guestbook?"

"Absolutely," he responded, and laid his business card down. I noted that his name was Edward Cramer. He was president of his real estate firm, Circle Realty in Tierrasanta, and that he was the ombudsman for the San Diego Association of Realtors. I was impressed that this nice-looking gentleman was president of his own firm.

The couple enjoyed my open house and although his clients liked the home, the back yard wasn't large enough. As they left, Mr. Cramer invited me to keep his business card and he grabbed a flyer about the house, which included my name and phone number. A week later, the phone rang. It was Edward Cramer. He said, "I've got a house in Tierrasanta that I'd like you to sell." He provided me with the specs.

"Mr. Cramer, I'd be honored," I responded. "Let me take a look at the property and get back to you." Which I did. Coincidentally, I had a couple who wanted to move to Tierrasanta and Ed's listing was perfect for them. We completed a smooth, swift and successful transaction. I liked the way he did business. He was honest, straightforward and professional. He, in turn, said he appreciated the same traits in me.

After escrow closed, he called me again, this time for a date.

Edward and Gigi on their wedding day; Gigi dancing with her sons, **Randall** and **Cameron**

Mom flew out several days before our wedding. The ceremony overlooked the Pacific Ocean at La Jolla Beach & Tennis Club on Saturday, August 13, 1994. Without my knowledge, Mom had purchased that gorgeous Geoffrey Beene designer wedding gown in Washington, D.C., after I accepted Ed's marriage proposal.

"Would you like to join me for dinner?" he inquired. I turned him down.

"That's very sweet of you to ask me, Edward," I said. "But I'm not dating right now. I've got my hands full with my two sons. They're both in competitive soccer and tennis, so I really don't have the time."

Fortunately, Edward persisted. At Christmas, 1990, he invited me to the Snow Ball at the San Diego Zoo. I gave in and agreed to accompany him. The evening was lovely. It turned out that we got along very, very well. I was quite taken. A retired commander in the U.S. Navy who had served nearly 26 years, Edward was an honest-to-goodness gentleman.

We started going out regularly and grew serious. One evening, he took me to the Marine Room in La Jolla for dinner where I met his three delightful daughters. I had the most wonderful time chatting with them. They were

Ed and I at The Old Globe Gala in the fall of 2013. Standing in front of the theatre in Balboa Park. It was to be the last Globe Gala we attended together.

all married with children of their own and all of them led fascinating lives. Over time, I fell in love with each of them. Ed and I married three years later at the La Jolla Beach & Tennis Club. I was so happy to inherit Ed's three daughters and he, my two sons. The perfect match!

Marrying Ed was one of the best decisions I've ever made. While we honeymooned in Hawaii, Ed asked me a mind-expanding question. Was I happy staying in real estate, or were there other choices I'd like to make, now that we had the freedom to explore the universe together? Never before had anybody asked me that question. The very idea of not having to continually worry about being the sole breadwinner took me aback. The Vietnam War gave Ed a passion to visit and understand more of the world and I was open to that. It was time for change and I also felt obligated to help those in need. I will always remember my mother's lessons – if you're not making a difference doing good in the world, what the heck are you doing here?

Together, we made plans to venture around the world and committed ourselves to a life of philanthropy.

CHAPTER 20

Rolling Readers

The causes closest to my heart are advocating for abused, abandoned and neglected children, supporting theater and the arts, healing the ocean and helping unwanted animals. My conviction toward the first was motivated by memories of my childhood. I wasn't abused during those years in the wonderfully kind Mrs. Yowell's basement. But I felt abandoned at times. I remain determined to offer my experience, strength, love and hope to the children who need it most.

I decided to hang up my real estate license and began to seek volunteer opportunities in my community to offer whatever support and resources I could contribute. I looked first to the local schools, volunteering in the front office of the high school for a couple of hours each week. Both my boys had attended Scripps Ranch High School and that seemed a good place to start. While there, I ran across an article in the school newspaper about an organization called Rolling Readers, where lay people would read to children in their classrooms. I had always read to my boys as they were growing up and knew how valuable this quiet bonding time was between us.

Close to Scripps Ranch High School was Walker Elementary School. They had begun their own program of Rolling Readers, and had an opening for a volunteer on Thursday mornings. The spot was for an ESL (English as a Second Language) class. I had no experience working with immigrants. But there I was, reading to a group of second- and third-graders, most of whom had come to California from Mexico, China, Singapore, South America and Africa, just to name a few places.

As I walked into the classroom for the first time, I was introduced to a remarkable teacher named Gwen Salter. She embodied the spirit of kindness and encouragement to this group of eager children, and I hoped to emulate that spirit in my reading. For five incredibly satisfying years, every week, I showed up in Gwen's classroom. The children responded to the way I was able to tell a story, and I felt an instant connection with them. They responded attentively to my energy, excitement and enthusiasm.

With Gwen's permission for each session, I dressed to reflect the content of my reading, as well as to observe the holidays throughout the year. On Easter, I came as the Easter Bunny. For Halloween, I dressed up as a witch riding a broom, but not too scary. I arrived as one of Santa's elves at Christmastime. I honored their home country holidays, too, recounting stories and wearing costumes related to their traditions.

At the end of each school year, I selected and gifted one book to every child, uniquely meaningful to him or her, encouraging them to read it over the summer. With a personal note on the inside cover of each book, I let them know how important it was for them to continue their reading, hopefully hearing my voice in the words on every page.

In all the classes I read to, I remember one child in particular who was raised in Rwanda. Kibibi, which means "princess," was a beautiful eight-year-old who had escaped her country's massacres. She and her brother witnessed their mother and father being murdered by the machetes of Hutu extremists. Instructed to run for their lives, she and her brother eluded the Hutu forces by hiding in the jungle. Her transition process, coming from Rwanda

DIAMOND GATEWAY SIGNATURE · OCTOBER 1999

SCHOOL NEWS

TOUCHING HER HEART- Gigi Cramer, cancer-survivor finds a wealth of happiness and satisfaction reading to students at Mira Mesa's Walker Elementary School's Rolling Readers Program. Shown here are Gwen Salter's second grade class. The Scripps Ranch mother is active in United Way/Chad and the American Cancer Society.

Survival of the fittest

Breast cancer survivor lives life to its fullest

By Gail Manginelli

Long-time Scripps Ranch resident Grace (Gigi) Cramer has not only been given a second chance at life, but a third.

And she's not about to waste a single minute.

First diagnosed with breast cancer in early 1991, the then 45-year-old single mother of two had most of her left breast removed after doctors detected a virulent carcinoma. Nine months later, a routine check-up revealed a not-yet-metastasized tumor under her left arm.

"Based on my first tumor that had spread so quickly, the doctors didn't want to take any chances," recalled Cramer. "They removed more tissue in my left breast, and I had regular follow-up visits for the next five years. In 1996, I was officially considered 'out of the woods,' and I've been celebrating ever since."

Cramer's zest for life is due in large part to her family: sons Randall Schiff, 21 and Cameron Schiff, 18, and second husband Ed, a real es-

'Sparkle,'" said Ed, "because she throws herself into everything with such energy, effervescence, enthusiasm and joie de vivre."

Active in yoga, aerobics classes and race-walking, Cramer is also a speaker for the American Cancer Society, United Way/Chad and the Wellness Community. She has been a deacon at Torrey Pines Christian Church for 17 years, and is a lifetime member of the American Association of University Women.

But it's reading to second and third graders at Mira Mesa's Walker Elementary School through the Rolling Readers Program that really touches Cramer's heart. "I could eat those kids alive, they're so precious. They help me realize how much joy, excitement and academic progress I can create just by reading words."

As one who has twice survived life-threatening diseases, Cramer's advice is simple, yet poignant. "Take time to nurture your mind, body and soul, they're very pre-

The following is an excerpt from an award-winning essay written in 1992 by Cramer's then 11-year-old son Cameron Schiff, in a contest sponsored by the La Jolla Cancer Research Foundation. Cameron's essay was placed in a time capsule to be opened in December 2092.

"I know I am just a little kid, and you probably think I don't know much about cancer, but you're wrong. I do, because my mom had breast cancer and she almost died.

You probably don't care what happens to my mom because you have too many other things to do, but I do care about my mom and anyone else who has cancer, and I hope that there is a cure for almost every cancer in the year 2000.

I hope you feel the same, because if we try hard enough, by the year 2000 I am sure that we will have more cures than we have now. So when you're working, think of what I said and you will work a lot faster. I promise."

to the United States, was unclear to me, but eventually, Bibi moved in with an aunt living close to the school.

When it was time for recess, Bibi often stayed behind. Once the other children left, Bibi would come over to me, put her arms around my legs, and we would hug one another for many minutes. I would tell her how precious she was, and repeat this sentiment to her over and over. She thanked me for being there, then joined the other children at recess.

At the end of the school year, Gwen had the kids write thank you notes to me. I received a card from every child. I have those cards to this day.

Of all the children I read to during my five years as a Rolling Reader, Bibi was my most special. She will always be my "princess."

After my fabulous five years as a Rolling Reader from 1995 to 2000, I continued my volunteer and philanthropic activities in the worlds of live theatre and child abuse prevention.

Dancing with Conrad

At the annual fall Globe Gala in 2014, I had a magnificent, unexpected and delightful dance with the incredibly generous philanthropist Conrad Prebys. I had attended without my husband that night because Ed was out of town. Conrad approached my table and inquired, "Gigi, I see the chair next to you is empty. Is Ed all right?" I replied, "He's finishing a real estate transaction in Northern California."

"Would you care to dance?" he said. I responded, "Oh, Conrad. I would be honored." He gallantly took my hand and we swooped out onto the ballroom floor. He was an elegant dancer. As soon as the waltz was over, I leaned in and whispered in his ear, "Conrad, San Diego will never ever be able to thank you for your amazing generosity. Everywhere I go, whether it's the Zoo, Sea World, UC San Diego, the Prebys Library or so many other institutions, you are always with us. Thank you for your phenomenal contributions to 'America's Finest City.'"

 I had the warmest admiration for Conrad and so did all of San Diego. The world lost that magnificent gentleman in 2016.

CHAPTER 21

Condom Diving and Other Thrills

Having a wonderful husband to share life with was an incredible blessing. Ed was as capable a father as possible to my sons, but raising 14- and 17-year-old teenagers presented a unique challenge for this tough military commander. The best times in our lives were all the trips we took together. My boys did not have much travel opportunity when we were The Three Musketeers and living solely on my income. But when we became a family of four, our lives blossomed!

In 1998, during high school spring vacation, Ed and I took Randall and Cameron to Oahu, Hawaii. One morning, the boys announced they were going kayaking. I told them that we would just relax and hang around in the condo until they got back. Four hours later, they returned, sporting wide grins as they unrolled scrolls congratulating them on their first skydiving adventure.

They didn't go kayaking. They went skydiving! Their eyes met mine hopefully, expecting me to be thrilled. However, I had an expression that didn't require any words at all. I was not happy.

"Mom," Randall said, "How can you be mad at us for skydiving?" Cameron was right on his heels, "Yeah, Mom. We didn't tell you we were skydiving because we were afraid you wouldn't want us to go."

"You better believe I'm angry," I said. They reacted as only teenage boys can, "Aw, Mom!"

"Now wait just a minute," I said. "The reason I'm angry is not because you didn't go kayaking. I'm upset because you didn't take me with you skydiving."

The very next day, the boys put me in our rental car and drove me up to Oahu's North Shore where I met my skydiving instructor. He sat me down to watch a 30-minute video, at the end of which I had to sign a waiver releasing the skydiving company from liability. The last thing he said to me as I stepped into the harness was, "You will be diving with an experienced and licensed skydiver. However, there is no such thing as a perfect plane, a perfect pilot, a perfect pupil, or a perfect parachute. Have fun!"

On the way to the airplane, Cameron instructed me that since I'd be flying with a certified instructor, the name of this technique is called "condom diving."

"Cameron," I laughed. "I think you mean tandem diving."

"Yeah, whatever," Cameron said.

"That's good, Son," I shot back. "At least you know about safe sex in the sky."

I cannot really explain what compelled me to step out of a perfectly good airplane at 15,000 feet. But I did and my tandem instructor and I free-fell at 120 mph for two minutes. When we pulled the ripcord, we were whisked even higher into the heavens. Once the parachute opened, we slowly and silently floated down to Earth. It was an indescribable feeling. For the first time in my life, I was truly flying!

Bungee jumping was even more exhilarating and frightening. Our next adventure was in New Zealand, where I decided to take one of those crazy giant rubber band jumps into the Shotover River on the South Island in Queenstown. After attaching me to the bridge with a complex network of harnesses, my instructor showed me how to dive going all the way down until my head touched the cresting waves of the river, which took all of six seconds. However, the adrenaline rush, punctuated by diving head first with a big band of elastic tied to my ankles, lasted for several days.

For his part, Ed declined participating in skydiving and bungie jumping. That notwithstanding, his parents had a passion for international cruising and had planted the travel seed in him. He loved cruise ships and I was fortunate enough to join him on many international travel escapades by sea.

Gigi and the bungee jumping episode

King Neptune baptism

Crossing the Arctic Circle halfway up the North Sea from Bergen, Norway, to Russia was another wonderful adventure. As a willing candidate and passenger aboard the *Hurtigruten*, a Norwegian cruise ship, I was "baptized" with a ladle of arctic water and ice cubes by our captain, who was portraying King Neptune. Very few passengers opted to engage in this chilling ceremony. Afterwards, I was given a cup of Gluhwein mulled wine to warm me up and was presented with an official Arctic Circle Crossing Certificate.

Coming south, on the way back to Norway, I was the only passenger crazy enough to have my Arctic Circle baptism a second time. This consisted of King Neptune again pouring ladles of icy arctic water down my back. Freezing half to death, both times, Ed remained on the aft deck. Watching me, he had serious doubts about my sanity. After skydiving, bungee-jumping and crossing the Arctic Circle, he wondered what other death defying challenges I had in mind.

Well, I had two more.

Scuba diving throughout the world deepened my passion for the oceans. My most favorite places to dive were Hawaii, British Virgin Islands, the Turks and Caicos (southeast of the Bahamas), the Canary Islands and Fiji. We went to the same beautiful location where Tom Hanks filmed *Castaway*. There's still the volleyball with Wilson's bloody handprint on display there. But my most engaging, yet frightening dive was the Great Barrier Reef adventure off the northeastern part of Australia. Sadly, the reef is under attack by warming waters, resulting in coral reef "bleaching." While diving, I witnessed this condition up close. Because of my love for the ocean, it was heartbreaking to see the damage being done to our exquisite coral reefs.

Scuba diving amidst Irukandji bloom

We arrived in Australia in the late spring, in the midst of an Irukandji bloom. I'd never heard of this small jellyfish, but learned that a sting from even one of their tiny babies is lethal.

There were 25 of us on the cruise. The dive coordinator separated us into two groups, snorkeling and scuba diving. He alerted us to the Irukandji bloom (a bloom is kind of an infestation) and warned us that these jellyfish are among the most deadly creatures on the planet. Their venom could kill a person within seven minutes. The weakened condition of the coral contributed to the increased population of the Irukandji. The dive coordinator put up a scrim so that the adult jellyfish couldn't get through the nets, but the babies could slither through.

Nobody from the group wanted to dive with these deadly sea creatures. Except one. Me.

I had to sign a three-page release of liability that guaranteed the dive promotors no responsibility. I was outfitted in a full diving body suit of lycra, a hood covering my head, gloves on my hands, boots on my feet and flippers. I also had my mask and buoyancy compensator. The only exposed part of me was my skin near the bottom of my face mask. As I swam, I saw these tiny, homicidal, gelatinous jellyfish right in front of me. At 65 feet down, I fed frozen peas to exotic fish, while observing man-eating clams at the same time that I pushed the little toxic jellies away.

I wasn't sure what overcame my senses at that time. Looking back, I still don't. Whatever the case, I managed to keep distance between me and deadly Irukandji stingers for the duration of my 60-minute dive. I came up, swam to the helicopter pad and changed clothes. Then, we took off over the Great Barrier Reef. As the 1,500-mile long stretch of natural art spread out before us, the sadness of the reef's declining condition was distinctly pressed into my heart and soul. These experiences kindled a fire in me to help heal these natural wonders. I passionately continue the fight to preserve the life of our cherished planet.

CHAPTER 22

The Path Between the Seas

As an anniversary present, Ed gave me a book by American historian David McCullough entitled *The Path Between The Seas*. Having been stationed in the Panama Canal Zone during his active duty, Ed wanted to return. This time, instead of sailing on a naval vessel, we decided to travel a little more luxuriously through the Panama Canal. It was important for him to show me a part of his life that he had not yet shared with me.

I looked at the book, saw it was 700 pages long, and said, "OK, I'll make you a deal. I will read this tome. I will go through the Panama Canal with you if we first head to Costa Rica and experience the Monte Verde zip lines through the triple canopies of Costa Verde." This is the highest and longest zip line in all of Latin America.

He acquiesced and I read the thick book. True to his word, he arranged our jungle lodging and I got to zip through the triple canopies amidst the lushest, thickest, most verdant vegetation I'd ever seen. And there was exotic wildlife, too – white faced capuchin monkeys, howler monkeys, toucans, two- and three-toed sloths, quetzals, coatis and a variety of living creatures indigenous to Costa Rica.

We then booked passage on a 14-day

ocean cruise ship through the National Trust for Historic Preservation. While underway, a helicopter landed on the aft deck. Out of the helicopter hopped none other than the author of *The Path Between The Seas*, David McCullough himself. It turned out he was going to lecture the next day and talk about the new book he was writing. That evening, he was scheduled to have dinner in the main dining hall of the cruise ship. Everybody on board was invited to that greatly anticipated event.

Switcheroo

I dressed early, made my way down to the dining room and found it empty. I did notice, however, that place cards were assigned to the seats. I scoped out ours. And I found David McCullough's. But we weren't at the same table. I took Ed's and my place cards off our table and put them next to David McCullough's. I mean, how many times do you have a chance to sit next to one of the most prominent historians in America?

I had done my homework on McCullough and knew he was researching a book he was calling, *Adams and Jefferson*. Given my history at William And Mary, I was very interested in his opinions about Thomas Jefferson. During our meal, I asked Mr. McCullough if he'd finished his book about Adams and Jefferson. He was surprised that I'd known about this pending manuscript and advised that he was nearing completion. However, when he said the title would be, *John Adams*, I almost dropped my wine.

"What about Jefferson?" I asked, incredulously. McCullough responded, "There are so many books in print about Thomas Jefferson. After doing my research, I found he wasn't all that fascinating." I would have begged to differ, but sometimes, discretion is the better part of valor. I kept quiet. But it was not the best dinner conversation I've ever had. I looked over at the people whose place cards I switched and wondered if they wanted to change seats.

A surprise call, Kissinger, Olympics and Hotel California

In 2003, Timothy J. Sullivan, the 25th president of the College of William and Mary, surprised me with a phone call. He informed me that I was being honored with the Alumni Service Award. President Sullivan flew out several weeks later with an entourage from William and Mary to make the presentation himself.

I still cherish that crystal award. In addition, I was delighted to learn that I was being inducted into the College of William and Mary's prestigious "Chancellor's Circle" the following year.

Twelve months passed and Ed and I flew to New York City to meet the Chancellor of the College of William and Mary, Dr. Henry Kissinger. A special reception and dinner were held at the Knickerbocker Hotel in Times Square. By the way, of the 13 Chancellor Circle inductees, I was the only female. While our circumstances were different, I couldn't help but think of my mother's pioneering medical school days where she was the only woman in a male-dominated arena.

Since I had travelled the farthest from coast to coast, Dr. Kissinger invited Ed and me to his table. His wife, Nancy, wasn't there, but he'd mentioned they'd married in Arlington, Virginia, in 1974 by a Justice of the Peace. Coincidentally, my first husband, Raymond, and I had been married by that same county official the year before, in 1973.

Four years later, at the Beijing Olympics, Ed and I ran into Dr. Kissinger again on August 8, 2008. Interestingly, in Asian culture, eight is a symbol of prosperity, money, health, etc. Kissinger remembered the pleasantries of our Knickerbocker encounter. We discussed the Olympics, amicable relations with China, and the progress the United States had made in international trade. It was lovely to see him again.

Gigi, Henry Kissinger and Ed

The trip was wonderful. The excitement and majesty of the ceremonies and competition are forever etched in my memory. But those weren't the most memorable parts of our journey.

While in Beijing, I wanted to explore the Great Wall of China. Ed and I walked to a cafe close to the Beijing entrance to the Great Wall and Ed had to sit down. The pollution in Beijing was thick and sooty, and he had trouble breathing. So he stayed inside the cafe while I paid several *yuan* to start climbing the Great Wall. As luck would have it, a group of uniformed Chinese students were also entering at the same time. These energetic young scholars were delighted to see a crazy white woman who was as curious as they were to explore a section of this world-famous and longest man-made architectural wonder, spanning over 13,000 miles. Although the students and I didn't speak the same language, we communicated beautifully as we laughed and had fun walking together. It turned into a very pleasant meeting of our very different cultures.

On another exciting adventure, Ed and I boarded the *China Princess* for a three-day cruise down the to Yangtze River to explore the Three Gorges Dam under construction. As we were boarding, I accidentally punctured my finger on a rusty nail protruding from the railing on the boat. I thought nothing of the puncture until three days later, when my finger was swollen and starting to throb. Alarmed, I detected a red line running from the end of my finger up my wrist. I kept soaking it every night in soapy, scalding hot water, and yet the red line continued to creep up my arm. It was showing every sign of septicemia – a life-threatening blood infection. Years earlier, Mother taught me about the severity of septicemia, a blood infection that could be life-threatening. If I hadn't taken care of it, it could have been fatal.

Seven days later, the red line was taking over my entire arm, accompanied by intensified pain. I decided to seek medical attention and went directly to the closest hospital once we were in Guilin, China, 19 hours from Beijing. Tour management arranged for a translator to drive me to the hospital. Upon arrival, I was confronted by a sea of more than 50 injured or sick people in the waiting room. There were no available seats, so the translator and I stood at the reception desk. He let the staff know why we were there, and then we found a place to stand in the waiting room, surrounded by locals suffering from a variety of urgent medical needs.

I glanced around this room and became concerned. I couldn't imagine how long the wait would be. To our pleasant surprise, within an hour, I heard someone yell, "Cramer." I looked at the translator and said, "What did you say to the staff?" He whispered three words – "wealthy white woman." You see, my translator had absolutely no concept of my financial status, but I was a guest in his country and he was responsible for my well-being. He wanted no negative publicity for China and knew the hospital staff would respond more quickly if they were aiding what they thought was a lady of means.

My translator and I were escorted down a long corridor to a surgical room. All the windows were open. It was none too clean and covered in flies. Further, every person in the room was smoking. It was hard to believe we were in a hospital.

The next person who appeared seemed to be a physician. His white coat was covered in blood. My translator let me know that this man had left a surgical procedure to come in to assist this "wealthy white woman." The doctor saw my tour name tag, which included my home town of San Diego, California, and said in heavily accented English, "Oh, you like Hotel California?" I replied, "By the Eagles?" He said, "Yes! I know that song."

He rolled over a flimsy little aluminum table, took my arm and poured Betadine solution all over my hand. It ran down the table, got all over my shoes and dripped onto the floor. He looked me in the eyes and queried, "What level pain tolerance?" I turned to my translator and said, "I had two natural childbirths without anesthesia, so I guess it's pretty high."

The doctor smiled, picked up a scalpel, and from my index fingernail, he drove the scalpel all the way down to the bone while singing "Welcome to the Hotel California." He tacitly indicated that he'd like me to sing along. You don't forget singing "Hotel California" with a blood stained Chinese surgeon who has driven a scalpel to the third joint of your index finger.

As tears streamed down my face, he scraped out all of the necrotic tissue and left a gaping open wound in my index finger. He then poured on more Betadine and loosely wrapped it in gauze, and said, "Must rinse every night. Wound stay open. Must heal from inside out."

Of all the adventures and excursions I've embarked upon, this provided a scar that is my most enduring "souvenir."

CHAPTER 23

Amazing Africa

I am a wildly fierce, conscientiously engaged and informed defender of animal rights. Therefore, I felt that it would be appropriate to visit Africa, home to some 1100 different species of mammals and more than 2,600 species of birds. In my research, I discovered more than 50 national parks and game reserves in Africa's 54 countries that offered tours, more commonly referred to as safaris, to see the wildlife populating different areas of this magnificent continent.

In 2010, Ed and I selected three safaris. The first was in South Africa – Krueger National Park – which had the most animals. The second safari was in Kalahari Game Reserve in Botswana, which hosted the most diverse range of creatures, including lions, cheetahs, elephants, rhinos and Cape buffalo – also famously known as "The Big 5." Lastly, we safaried at the Maasai Mara in Kenya, where we saw the annual game migration of the wildebeest, or gnu, a member of the antelope family.

More importantly, I was drawn to each of these countries because within their borders were orphanages where countless children had suffered the deaths of their parents from the HIV and AIDS epidemic. It is from listening to my mother that I arrived at this emotional space in my life. I felt that my greatest accomplishments would be judged by how much I could provide for and intervene on behalf of needy children. Fortunately, I had packed my suitcase with many treats, like packages of Lifesavers, hopefully providing a safe, welcoming introduction.

Before visiting several orphanages, I had this burning desire to take a microlight flight over Victoria Falls, "the smoke that thunders" – the largest sheet of falling water anywhere in the world. From Zambia to Zimbabwe, we glided over flocks of hippos whose babies were resting on the backs of their mothers. There were also storks protecting their young in acacia and baobab trees. At the end of the flight, we had lunch in a field, surrounded by wild zebras. As much as I wanted to pet these gorgeous striped animals, I had to remember they were not tame!

When we arrived in Zimbabwe, I arranged for a translator to take us to an orphanage, where I encountered dozens of abandoned children. For the first moments, we stood silently, locking eyes. I was awed and heartbroken by their presence. Then, I slowly reached into my bag and pulled out handfuls of what they considered extraordinary gifts – packages of Lifesavers hard candy. I handed one to each child, while asking the translator to tell them I cared, that they mattered, and that Lifesavers were symbols of redemption and hope. This small gesture was only a minute token of my deep feelings for them. With the sweet candy on their tongues, the children old enough to understand my translated words began crying. Tears rolled down my cheeks, too. I'm not sure who was crying more.

In return, their gift to me was a reinforced foundation of firm resolve to assist children's charities for the rest of my life.

As we left the company of these precious orphans, my husband and I explored Soweto, Cape Town and Durban. Nelson Mandella was from Soweto, and Durban was home to Mahatma Ghandi for 21 years. Ed and I were humbled to attend an annual ritual birthday celebration in Ghandi's house. A framed parchment plaque hanging from the front door caught my attention as I was walking up the front stairs. I lingered long enough to commit its quotation to memory – "Live as if you could die tomorrow. Learn as if you could live forever." What a powerful way of expressing how very important it is to live life to the fullest and make the most of every moment.

Family portrait taken at Cameron's UC San Diego John Muir School of Economics graduation, June 16, 2012. Ed (far left) and I took Cameron, his then fiancé, Katie, and Randall to the University Club in downtown San Diego following commencement. Because our family loves Hawaii, we gave him an orchid lei to celebrate this very special occasion.

In 2015, Ghandi's quote and, really, all of the truth, wisdom, knowledge and character I had acquired in my first 69 years, was severely put to the test. But that is getting ahead of the story. Before the dramatic, life-altering events of 2015, both my sons graduated from college and my younger one got married.

Two graduations and a wedding

As did my mother before me, I value higher education and did everything in my power to impart that value on my two sons. I am pleased to say they picked up on my cues and each is academically accomplished. On June 12, 2009, Randall graduated from U.C. San Diego Warren School of Science and Engineering.

Randall's 2009 graduation plaque

Cameron followed in his big brother's continuing education footsteps and attended U.C. San Diego John Muir School of Economics. He graduated on June 16, 2012. That same year, he met his future wife, Katie. Two years later, Cameron and Katie married at the beautiful facilities at the Point Loma Naval Base.

After the graduations and wedding, Ed and I were ready to take on the world.

Then, the worst happened.

Cameron's 2012 graduation portrait

Cameron and Katie's wedding, March 29, 2014

PART II
What's it Like to Die?

"There are only two ways to live your life.
One is as though nothing is a miracle.
The other is as though everything is a miracle."

Albert Einstein

CHAPTER 24

Super Bowl Sunday

As I mentioned in the *Introduction*, on Super Bowl Sunday, February 1, 2015, the last thing I told my wonderful Edward was, "Oh, my God, Sweetheart, we're going to die." And yes, we did die.

Up until the moment of the horrific car crash, we'd had a magnificent few days together. Edward and I spent the weekend at the California Association of Realtors Convention at the Marriott Marquis in Palm Springs, attended by thousands of our state's real estate agents and brokers. The weather was perfect. We attended presentations, lunches, afternoon gatherings and breakout sessions over three days. Afterwards, we packed up, got in the car, drove toward home and made a couple of casual stops along the way.

I had driven to Palm Springs on Friday, January 29, so Ed decided to drive us back home February 1. Our trip was relaxing and everything was going along beautifully. I lounged in the passenger seat and dozed off. All of a sudden, I felt the car speeding up, speeding up, speeding up! I opened my eyes and realized we were barreling down the offramp at Mira Mesa Boulevard and hurtling through four lanes of traffic. I glanced at my husband, who was slumped over the steering wheel. He had either passed out or died. His foot was jammed down on the accelerator. I uttered my final words to him and screamed as we slammed into a 35-foot steel traffic pole at 70 miles per hour.

Everything went black.

I recall nothing of the following three months. I later learned that two ambulances were called to the scene. The entire front of Ed's Lincoln Town Car had been totally pushed backward and the vehicle nearly exploded. The engine burst through the dashboard and shattered almost every bone in my body. The EMTs took us to Scripps Hospital. With Ed sprawled over the steering wheel, his chest was totally crushed upon impact. Despite their best efforts, the trauma team couldn't even find Ed's heart, much less revive him. I wouldn't learn the truth of his fate for quite a while.

I, in turn, was bleeding out and had stopped breathing. My seatbelt virtually cut me in half, blowing out both my spleen and gallbladder. It had crushed my lower rib cage so that tiny bone fragments punctured both my left & right lungs (causing COPD for the rest of my life). It also lacerated both my liver and pancreas. My cervical, thoracic and lumbar vertebrae were shattered. Even my left arm and hand were broken. My prospects were grim. Representatives of the trauma unit called my sons to advise them that Ed and I were in a catastrophic car accident and both boys should come to the hospital immediately. No other details were disclosed over the telephone.

Because of the severity of my injuries, the trauma team put me in a medically-induced coma, during which time, the opioids Dilaudid, fentanyl and oxycodone were pumped into my system. At first, the doctors were not at all optimistic, saying I had less than a four percent chance of survival. Countering their assertion, Cameron stood up straight and tall, put his hands on his hips and stated, "Gentlemen, you don't know my mother. She's a fighter. She's going to pull through."

Even though I was in a coma, my subconscious was working overtime. I distinctly recall floating down a lighted corridor, silently and miraculously pain-free. It was the most ethereal feeling. I looked down below me and observed a gurney with a pathetic, twisted body, ugly and bleeding everywhere. I didn't recognize that figure. I saw physicians working desperately to save this person. Who could that poor victim be?

I continued traveling silently inside a lighted passageway. I had no physical sensation whatsoever. As I look back on it, I realized I was floating above my body. But I had been lifted out of my physical state through the silver cord (Ecclesiastes 12:6).

> **Ecclesiastes 12:6**
>
> Or ever the silver cord be loosed, or the golden bowl be broken, or the pitcher be broken at the fountain, or the wheel broken at the cistern.

Then, for the first time, I thought, "Hey, maybe that body is me." It didn't bother me. I felt nothing. It simply was. I figured I was going to Heaven.

Then, jarringly, I wasn't moving upward. I was headed down a long corridor that was getting smaller and darker. I was profoundly frightened as the corridor became more cramped. I asked myself, "Why am I not going into the light? I know I have to go to the light because I have to go see God. What's happening?"

A few feet ahead of me, I noticed what looked like a crowd of people gathered at the end of the corridor. As I got closer, the crowd took on the appearance of mannequins, disguised with pieces of charcoal colored fabric over their faces. When I got close enough, I grabbed an arm, thinking it was a family member. I looked at the figure's face. I recognized no one. I absolutely panicked. "Who are these creatures? If I'm not going to Heaven, am I going to Hell?"

I still wasn't in any physical pain, but I remained in a dark, profoundly lonely blur. Evidently, I wasn't Heaven-bound. I crashed back into my body and screamed in agony. I think that was after my trauma surgeons finally had success with multiple firings of the defibrillation paddles. I was back and that's when I felt the excruciating pain return. I was alive and it hurt like hell. Then came the bizarre dreamscape of a drug-induced coma.

Meanwhile, my boys were devastated. Since there was nothing they could do for me at the moment, they went to the ocean for comfort. Throughout their lives, when they needed clarity, they both surfed themselves to exhaustion on the demanding waves of the mighty Pacific. That day, Cameron – not a particularly religious man, but very spiritual – made a promise to The Almighty. He prayed, "Lord, if you could see your way clear to allowing Mother to live, I promise you, Sir, that I will change careers. I will leave retail and go into the medical profession. Just as my grandmother did, I will save lives."

Randall committed to my recovery in his own way. In the next chapters, I will explain his critical role in preparing my home for my return.

To help me heal as quickly as possible, both boys knew that the sounds of the ocean would be soothing to me. Randall and Cameron went to the beach again and recorded the crescendo of the ocean waves, the wind and seagull cries, and transferred the soundtrack to a CD. They asked the trauma staff to play the ocean CD for me as frequently as possible.

The sea is my lifeline. I have been a supporter of Ocean Conservancy International for decades. Later, my sons told the Conservancy about my accident, and they emphasized that I recovered more quickly because of those transformative sounds of the sea. Thanks to my sons, even in my comatose state, I could hear this life-sustaining presence every afternoon.

NIL DESPERANDUM

Hawkins

Family History

Hawkins

Cameron's big brother by three years is Randall Hawkins Schiff. His middle name represents a nod back to 1588, when Spain had ruled the seas. By the mid-16th Century, the English became increasingly exasperated with Spanish trade route domination. Right around then, my relative, Englishman Sir John Hawkins, cousin to Sir Francis Drake, played a key role in overcoming the enormous Spanish galleons, using lighter, swifter, more agile boats. In the autumn of 1588, with the help of a violent three-day storm off the shores of England, John and Francis led forces to disable and scuttle the Spanish Armada. After this great victory, Queen Elizabeth I knighted the pair in 1588. I am a **proud** direct descendant of Sir John Hawkins.

Guins

On the Guin side, I am descended from the French Huguenots – a Protestant religious sect in Paris, France, which adhered to Calvinism. "Guin" was pronounced "Gan" in France. Between 1640 and 1650, being a Protestant in predominantly Catholic Paris was not good for one's health. Back then, citizens were given a choice – "Convert to Catholicism or you'll be decapitated and your head will be placed on a spike and displayed around Parisian churches and cathedrals." Some of these Protestants opted to stick with their religious beliefs, but hightailed it to the Americas where they settled in several parts of this country, including Kentucky, Alabama and Tennessee.

My French Huguenot relatives came to Alabama, right outside Birmingham. Another family of my bloodline settled in Tennessee and changed their name to Crockett. In fact, Davy Crockett is my six times great uncle. Uncle Davy doesn't really play too much into my story other than that I gave my son, Cameron, the middle name, Crockett.

CHAPTER 25

Nil Desperandum

My boys kept faith that I would recover. Every day, Randall was at my bedside, whispering, "Mom, remember – *Nil Desperandum!*" Over and over, he repeated the words from the stunning Hawkins Coat of Arms painting that Mother had commissioned so many years earlier and that they grew up seeing. *Nil Desperandum.* It is our family motto — "Never give up, never despair."

The medical team, on the other hand, didn't share my sons' optimism. Yet, after 10 weeks in my medically-induced coma, a trauma surgery team representative contacted both Randall and Cameron.

"It's a miracle," he marveled. "Your mother is going to make it. She is one tough lady. I guess you know that. It will require months of rehabilitation, but your mother will survive. The entire trauma team has named her 'Miracle Warrior.'"

Hearing this news, Cameron jumped into his car and drove directly to Kohl's Department Store where he was employed as a store manager. He proffered his two-week resignation and promptly made his way up to PIMA Medical Institute in north San Diego County to enroll in a medical education program.

Randall gave me a year of his life, first readying my residence for my return, reconfiguring the floor plan so I could live independently. After I finally returned home, he stayed in my guest room, helping me at every turn. Randall gave me back my home, my sanctuary. It's because of Randall that I have peace of mind knowing that I will always have my cherished home in Scripps Ranch. I don't know what I would have done without him – without either of my loving and compassionate sons.

Awakening

When I emerged from my 10-week coma, Randall was sitting next to my bed. He saw me stir. As he peered at me, I opened my eyes and, looking back at him, uttered five syllables – words that had been repeated to me over and over throughout my unconscious ordeal.

"*Nil Desperandum,*" I muttered, barely audibly. But he was leaning in and heard me. He squeezed my hand, and through his tears, whispered, "Mom, you're back."

Over the next two weeks, I regained my senses. The trauma team paid close attention to my progress, preparing for the next phase of my treatment. The plan was that I would be discharged from the hospital and begin rehabilitation at a different facility.

The hours moved so slowly after I awoke. The passing of time was once again ethereal. I couldn't move my head from side to side and had no idea why. I focused on the ceiling for all my waking hours. I couldn't walk— I couldn't leave my bed. And even though I was on the best drugs available, the pain remained fearsome.

When I was vaguely coherent, they gave me the news that my dear Edward had died in the accident. In a moment, my world came crashing down. Again. But I knew I had to gather strength amidst debilitating grief to move forward, for the sake of my sons and for my sake – for the sake of *Nil Desperandum*. I called on my faith to sustain me, and I called on it non-stop.

Chasing the dragon

Scripps Memorial's Trauma Center professionals continued my surgeries on what seemed to be a daily basis. My body had been broken, shattered and crushed almost beyond repair. Twenty-three gifted trauma surgeons took turns applying their scalpels and working their magic. I'm forever indebted to every last one of them for giving me back my life.

Coming to after one of those surgeries, I felt an intense hurt sear through my chest. I screamed. I turned bright red and couldn't catch my breath. The nurse rushed in and asked me what was wrong. I said, "I have a horrible pain in my chest."

They put me on a gurney and rolled me out to an elevator and up to a surgery floor. They conjectured I was either having an aneurysm or a heart attack. The only pain even close to this was during the car accident, when the seatbelt nearly ripped me in half, lacerating my liver and pancreas and destroying my gallbladder and spleen.

The doctors wanted to observe me to determine what the cause of my pain might be and decided I should be given a shot of something that disconnected me from my body. My mind was barely alert – it felt close to being in a conscious drunken state. My body felt detached, as if it didn't belong to me, and I entered euphoria. I went to places in my mind I'd never been to before. I remember the dark, the quiet, the images, but mostly, the awareness of being pain-free.

I went on a journey to paradise and was overcome by a sense of bliss. "Bliss" is the only word I can assign to this physical state that offers even a modicum of insight into what was a profoundly saturated sense of enraptured pleasure. I don't know how long it lasted, but I remember the exact moment of the pain's return. I was so eager to hang on to every last vestige of this extraordinary physical relief that I begged the nurse to give me one more shot. Digging my fingernails into her arm, I pleaded with her to do anything in her power to stop the pain before it consumed me once again.

The nurse calmly removed my fingernails from her arm, leaned over and whispered, "Mrs. Cramer, you only get one." I desperately wanted to return to my place of bliss, but that wasn't going to happen ever again.

Several days later, the boys came to visit and I described in detail the experience I had while under observation for that crippling chest pain. I told them exactly how the agony had disappeared, offering a floating, disconnected physical state. And I told them how badly I wanted that experience to be a permanent part of my life, not merely a moment in my rehabilitation.

Randall and Cameron patiently listened. When I was through, they paused for a moment and Randall offered, "Well, Mom, we hate to break this to you, but that is generally referred to as 'chasing the dragon.' You hear this with people who have experienced any kind of opiate for the first time. Heroin users will tell you how their pain is drawn up into a very manageable and almost unrecognizable form, only to come back and require the user to administer the drug more frequently with a stronger dose."

For me, I wanted to return to that state of euphoria. I have never had another experience like it. I was never given another shot of that magnitude. But the doctors continued to prescribe opiates.

The Physician's Perspective

Imad S. Dandan, MD,
FACS, Trauma, Critical Care and Acute Care Surgery,
Scripps Memorial Hospital La Jolla

Dr. Dandan

To the world at large, Dr. Imad S. Dandan is a gifted and dedicated trauma surgeon.
To Gigi's family, he is nothing short of the hero who saved their mother's life.

On February 1, 2015, the good doctor was on his usual trauma 24-hour shift at Scripps Memorial
Hospital--La Jolla when he was notified that a couple was arriving by ambulance. They'd been in
a serious car crash. A deadly crash, as it turned out. As chief of trauma, critical care and acute
care surgery, Dr. Dandan immediately led his skilled team into action.

"We heard Gigi's screams from the ER long before we ever saw her. She was covered in blood and obviously
experiencing excruciating pain. She was hollering about how she couldn't breathe. But triage is a critical component of
trauma care and her husband arrived in cardiac arrest, far worse off than she. The trauma team spent an hour trying
to bring him back. But unfortunately, it was too late."

continue ⟶

Then Dr. Dandan focused his full attention on Gigi.

"She was alive, awake and talking. As her trauma surgeon, I took care of her in totality." Trauma care is a team sport, where physicians, nurses and specialists work together to help patients. Over the following three months, 23 physicians were called upon to be part of the team. Gigi was also an essential part of that team.

"Gigi had been nearly cut in half by the seatbelt. We stratified her injuries, determining what could kill her, what could maim her, and lastly, what were more cosmetic injuries, such as lacerations. First of all, we had to address the prolific bleeding in her abdomen. Her spleen had ruptured, too, as had her gallbladder. We removed both. Additionally, both her liver and pancreas were lacerated, neither of which can be removed. We packed around those vital organs to stay the bleeding and transferred her to the radiology suite, where we inserted special plugs in her liver arteries to stop the bleeding entirely. At that time, her abdomen was packed open — meaning we used special devices to keep everything inside, but her abdomen was exposed. Two days later, after ensuring the bleeding had stopped, we removed the packing and closed her abdomen. Eventually, her liver regenerated itself, but Gigi now lives with a smaller pancreas and is susceptible to type 1 diabetes, due to reduced insulin production.

"If asked then, would I have conjectured she would live? The answer would have been a resounding NO! The more we examined her, the more critical problems we discovered. Truly, none of us on duty could imagine how anyone in Gigi's condition could survive. Not only did she have extensive multiple injuries, but each was life-threatening. Still, we always do everything in our power to preserve life and that's what we set about doing.

"Gigi's injuries meant she had less than 4% chance of survival. A woman of her age at that time (69) – not old, but the biggest enemy of trauma injury survival after age 55 is, well, age. The breaking point is 55 and sustaining life after that age is greatly lessened. Considering all that, she is a warrior, a child...whatever you want to call her. She surprised us around every corner. Every time we did something big and assumed it would hit her hard, she overcame.

"Also, there were multiple orthopedic injuries that had to be addressed. Gigi's right leg was totally shattered. Dr. Richard Thunder, Chief of Orthopedic surgery, led the efforts to save and rebuild her damaged limb. Others handled therapy for her crushed left arm (radius ulna), left wrist and all of the fingers on her left hand.

"Dr. Scott Leary was Gigi's neurosurgeon, who addressed her shattered cervical, thoracic and lumbar vertebrae. He shaved her head, placed a steel plate up against her skull and bolted four steel rods to her skull, thus allowing her to sit and stand up straight. The rods prevent her from driving because she can't look up, down or side to side without turning her entire body. Then again, she has terrific posture today.

"But these are only a few of the more than 100 procedures performed on Gigi by 23 talented surgeons and dozens of medical professionals to literally put this feisty lady back together again.

"We had to control her pain AND her breathing. To understand what she was going through, try to imagine a tube the size of your thumb lodged down your throat 24 hours a day. That's not very comfortable. To help her relax, we put her into a medically-induced coma, where the patient isn't awake. Gigi was on general anesthesia for a long period of time. That state helped her heal because she wasn't fighting the breathing tube or her body's natural tendency to breathe on its own. The deep sleep diverted her energy into healing."

While Gigi lay unconscious for 10 weeks, she received mountains of well-wishing cards, phone calls and prayers from family and friends. Dozens of people tried to visit her, but were turned away at the door because the medical staff wanted to protect her from the possibility of infection outsiders might carry in. In fact, the only people allowed at her bedside were her sons and daughter-in-law, who conveyed all the prayers, well wishes and concern from her friends. Did all those prayers affect her outcome? Dr. Dandan says yes.

"The power of prayer is medically proven." Prayers provide comfort. We talk to the patients and ask the family to talk to them, too. We don't really know if they hear – there is no way of telling that. In any case, prayer helps calm the patient so they can rest and heal.

"Further, the patient's attitude plays a huge role. If he or she gives up, there's really little that can be done. He's seen this happen many times in his life and career.

"Fortunately, Gigi is not a quitter. It's like she said, 'Hell no, I'm not going.'"

continue ⟶

After she woke up and Dr. Dandan spoke with her, he came to understand her personality, her fighting spirit and, as he defined it, "Her spunkiness. After that, everything fell into place as to how she overcame her injuries. I thought, 'Okay, that's the person who will survive.' Just look at her smile!"

The ICU nurses nicknamed Gigi "Miracle Warrior." Dr. Dandan concurred, adding that in a twist of fate, the ICU where he and others began life-saving efforts for Gigis right next to the NICU (Neonatal Intensive Care Unit) where her son, Cameron, now works as a respiratory therapist.

Every December, the hospital hosts a celebration for all trauma patients Dr. Dandan and his team have saved. In 2015, he recalls pushing her up to the podium in her wheelchair where "She took the mic and went on like a house-afire talking about how phenomenal all the trauma team had been. But the fact of the matter is, whether or not she's singing our praises, we always love seeing her in street clothes…alive, well and thriving."

CHAPTER 26

Liberation to Purgatory

I never thought it would happen, but Liberation Day arrived at last. Every one of my physicians gave the green light. They called my sons and said that I would be discharged within the week. The boys, of course, were overjoyed. So was I.

Over the next few days, I allowed myself the joy of reveling, thinking, "This is it! I'm done with throwing up, blood clots, pulmonary embolisms, deep vein thromboses, interventions and all those nasty procedures they mention on silly television commercials. I'm free!" Little did I know, the hard part was yet to happen.

The ambulance showed up with the world's best EMTs to escort me to my new home. These guys had already given me lots of rides to different specialists, checking on my liver regeneration. Also, my neurosurgeon needed X-rays of all four steel rods bolted to my skull that go all the way down to my pelvis. It was critical these rods remained completely stable. Equally important were the return trips to Scripps ordered by Dr. Thunder, Chief of Orthopedic Surgery, to monitor the progress of my shattered and rebuilt right leg. While the EMTs expertly transferred me from bed to gurney and back again, we'd joke and laugh the whole time. Oh, okay, it didn't hurt that they happened to be good-looking young men. I was broken – not dead.

Diabolical muscle machines

In preparation for Liberation Day, Cameron and my good friend, Elaine, toured five rehabilitation facilities. They identified Villa Rancho Bernardo as the most well-equipped and best staffed in San Diego. They loved it for two very good reasons, both of which, of course, I detested. First of all, it had the most arduous gym in the world, featuring more diabolical muscle strengthening machines than I could have imagined in my worst nightmares. The second reason was how rigorously the therapists worked with patients, hours and hours a day.

My boys had made arrangements ahead of time, dotting every last "i" and crossing every single "t" to enroll me in my new temporary home. They escorted me to my room on the first floor, to the bed by the window with a view of the beautiful rose garden. I thought it would be lovely if I could look out on that scene every day.

However, the cost of all my medical bills became a persistent worry, swirling amidst my other concerns. Was I ever going to leave rehab? Was I going to have to sell my house – what in the name of God was I going to do if I had to leave my wonderful home in San Diego? Would I ever walk again? I'd barely had time to settle in when the director blew in with stacks of papers for me to sign and a medicine cabinet full of pills for me to take. She issued her marching orders like a drill sergeant. Her demeanor clued me in on what kind of purgatory I was entering. Later, the evening crew started and yet another nurse advised me, "It's almost time for dinner, Mrs. Cramer, and we have your heparin shot."

"What do you mean, heparin shot?" I said, dismayed. "I thought I was done with all that."

"Oh, no, ma'm. You had thrown so many blood clots and deep vein thromboses while you were at Scripps that we will continue injecting the blood thinner into your abdomen. One dose in the morning, one in the afternoon."

Oh my God, here we go again. You see, along with its medicinal benefit, heparin has dreadful side effects on me. Pain, dizziness, vomiting… the list goes on. It was then that I became acutely aware of what was really happening. Although under a new roof, my hospital nightmares would continue. They'd still check vitals. There would be blood draws and weigh-ins. Further, despite my lack of appetite, I was advised in no uncertain terms, "You will have breakfast, you will have lunch, and you will have dinner." Next came the part about working with both a physical therapist (PT) and an occupational therapist (OT) three hours a day, six days a week.

I'm here to tell you, the cuisine left much to be desired. Sure, meals were nutritious enough, but absolutely unimaginative. They served watermelon for lunch and dinner. Watermelon, watermelon, and occasionally, cantaloupe. Apparently, Villa Rancho Bernardo chefs were unaware that any other fruits existed.

One bright spot in all of this was my night duty nurse. She was adorable. She introduced herself to me, and inquired, "Mrs. Cramer, what is your pain level?" I thought, "What do you mean, what's my pain level? Nobody has ever asked me that before. They didn't ask me that at the hospital. None of my trauma surgeons, and there were 23 of them, ever inquired what my stupid pain level was." While I was thinking all this and looking at her incredulously, she tried again, "Well, on a scale of one to ten, with ten as the worst, what is your pain level?"

"What?" I exclaimed. "I only get one to ten? My pain level goes from 45 to 50 freaking thousand." You can imagine, she was taken aback. I guess she considered me a lady, incapable of rough language. Well, Mother raised me to be polite, but somehow or another, I couldn't handle the "one to ten" thing. It was beyond frustrating.

Still, she acted lovingly and in her kind ways, gently got through to me. We became good friends. I tempered my profanity around her. But I was still upset at having been whisked away from the trauma center at Scripps, only to find myself in this hellhole. Rehab regimen was miserable. The worst part of all was that the lights came on every morning between 6:45 and 7:00 a.m. I didn't do mornings well when I was home, and I sure as heck was not doing terribly well in rehab at that early hour, either.

"Good morning, Mrs. Cramer! This is your wake up call. Breakfast will be here in 15 minutes. You better hurry up and get dressed." Hell, I couldn't hurry up and do anything. Everything was too broken, shattered, crushed and fractured. What was this "get dressed" crap? I couldn't even walk.

By 7:15, after I had attempted breakfast, they wrestled me into some kind of a warm-up outfit so I could be wheeled into the diabolical gym. Those daily three-hour workouts were misery incarnate.

More bad news

Just when I thought it wouldn't get worse, I learned that I would never get behind the wheel of a car again. My surgeons had done a phenomenal job of rebuilding my shattered body. Yet my cervical, lumbar and thoracic vertebrae had been so horribly damaged that I would never again have the flexibility to operate a car. I was a lady who had always had the freedom and independence to race downstairs, grab the keys, back out of my driveway, and go wherever on the planet I needed to go. Now I would be dependent on others to take me to family events, galas, lunches, dinners, plays, movies and places as mundane as grocery stores.

Admittedly, the team of therapists at Villa Rancho Bernardo were five-star, every single one of them. Unfortunately, I wasn't in a very loving, caring or compassionate mood when I realized that I would never again have the freedom to leave my home on my own. Thank God, I have two precious sons to inspire me. I also have wonderful friends, many of whom came to visit me while I was in rehab. I am forever grateful for their company and companionship.

When I started to think about recovery, reality hit me hard. If I ever get out of here, I thought, I will return to an empty house. I'm now a widow, all alone, and housebound for the rest of my life. But that wasn't the full extent of my challenge. Due to the introduction of so many drugs into my system for such a long period of time, I had become opioid dependent.

CHAPTER 27

The Three Million Dollar Woman

Due to the opioids, my subconscious imagination was alive and well. I would pass the hours traveling in a drug-induced haze, wondering, "When are my boys coming?" and "When do I get my next pill?" I was so broken and fragile when I first arrived at Villa Rancho Bernardo that my care team determined I couldn't receive visitors. Drugs became my only escape from pain. My sons were all the emotional support I had. As time passed and my condition improved, the doctors removed my "lockdown" status. Instantly, friends, church companions and people from every one of my charities rushed to my bedside, bringing much-needed gifts of bright flowers, delectable fruit juices and delicious (non-watermelon) fresh fruit. Further, I received stacks upon stacks of cards and letters — some sympathy for Ed's passing, others, well-wishes for my health. I know that my recovery was accelerated because of all these wonderfully caring people providing companionship and love, and convincing me that I was getting better day by day. These precious friends brought the world to me since I felt totally incarcerated.

Too many numbers

When people are so close to death that doctors put them in virtual isolation because of their bodies' condition, it gets very lonely. And scary. Not too unlike my childhood days in the Yowells' basement. But I got through it only to receive another shock to my system. Toward the middle of rehab, I received an envelope from Scripps Memorial Hospital's billing department. In bold print on the front were emblazoned the words "Please Pay Promptly." Curiosity and a vague sense of dread seized me. Trembling, I ripped it open, unfolded the invoice and stared. There were lots and lots of numbers. I tried to make sense of "....two hundred ninety-nine"...no wait...too many numbers. Two thousand something...Oh my God, is that thousands or millions?

Because of the effects of the oxycodone, I couldn't figure out what the numbers added up to. I focused with all my might. After about 15 minutes, I realized that my fees were nearly $3 million. $2,987,000 and some change. It utterly blew my mind. I hysterically screamed at The Almighty, "How much is a human being worth, Lord? What is my true value?" I cried myself to sleep that night and every night for the next seven weeks. What could I do? I had nothing but a lousy hospital gown, a wheelchair, lots of meds and a godawful bill looming over my bed. Oh, yes, and now I'm a widow without a partner. I didn't have that kind of money then, now or ever. I screamed up to the ceiling to The Lord every single night — "Where are you?" I prayed to die for almost two months.

One night, a nurse came in and asked, "Mrs. Cramer, what's your pain level?" I looked at her and grumbled, "Let me tell you, it's not really good today." And she responded by saying, "One 10-milligram Oxy, or two?" I said, "I'll take all you've got." She gave me two, and I lay there crying for hours. I didn't eat dinner that night. I didn't want to do anything. I didn't want to be here, there or anywhere. I didn't want to live.

Mixed up by oxycodone and terror, I went to bed that night pretty sure that the Scripps doctors were going to come over to my home under the cover of darkness, take a long nail and hammer my front door with an eviction notice. For the rest of the night, I thought I'd have to sell my home and steal a shopping cart to roll my few belongings throughout the city. I would be a homeless widow for the rest of my life, dwelling in San Diego's canyons. Alone and on my own, because I don't have $3 million. I was so upset that as I tried to sleep that night, I had nightmares. Three of them. They were bad – really bad.

What color wine?

In the first nightmare, I called both of my sons to my bedside. They took seats on two chairs, with Randall on one side and Cameron on the other. And I said, "Gentlemen, I want you to do me a favor. Go to the grocery store and buy a dozen bottles of wine. Then visit the pharmacy and purchase all their sleeping pills. Come back to me and open up each of the bottles of sleeping pills and wine. I'm going to take a pill and have a sip of wine. And then, I'm gonna take another pill and have another sip of wine. And so on."

In reality, I'm either such a coward or else I'm not a coward at all. I know I could never commit suicide because it would involve pain of some kind. And I also believe in the sanctity of life. In my dream, however, I figured if I downed sleeping pills with wine, I would fall asleep, never to wake up again.

During the nightmare, my boys returned with the wine and pills and I explained my plan to them. They were very quiet. And I said, "Any questions?" And Cameron said, "Mom, only one."

"Certainly, Honey. What is it?"

"What color wine?"

And at that point, the three of us burst out laughing. I realized what a stupid, idiotic idea that was. Then I woke up, sort of, only to fall back into another opiate-induced nightmare. It began with gathering the boys to my bedside again to announce in a stage whisper, "Guys, I can't take it anymore. I don't have $3 million. I can't pay this bill. And I just have too much pride to roll a grocery cart containing my lifelong belongings into a canyon and be a homeless broad. That's not the lady Mother raised me to be."

"I have a much better idea," my dreaming self continued. Randall said, "OK, what is it this time, Mom?"

"You know my Lexus Sport Coupe? Go get it and sneak me the heck out of Villa Rancho Bernardo. Come around back and we'll escape before they lock up for the night. Then, I want you to drive me to the top of the Coronado Bridge. Put me in the driver's seat, duct tape my hands to the steering wheel in case I change my mind. Then, push my car over the edge of the bridge into the bay. My sons were silent until once again I repeated, "Any questions?"

Never missing a beat, Cameron spoke up, "Mom? I don't mind pushing you over the bridge, but I love that little Lexus." The real-life Cameron would never have said such a thing, but in my nightmare haze, everything was made hideously bizarre by the drugs.

In the third and final nightmare, I found myself staring out the window, feeling bored and depressed. I wondered, "How much longer am I going to be here?" On cue, the boys came to visit me and wanted to take me to Torrey Pines Christian Church, where I was a lead deacon. But I told them I wanted to go, instead, to a Catholic church for an exorcism. I felt that, in my dream, this was the only way I would be relieved from all of my pain. One of the boys said, "Mom, you're not Catholic." I replied, "That's really not important to me. Take me to a Catholic church to see a priest and get this pain out of me." I was convinced that the devil had possessed me and was brutally torturing me. If that continued, I knew I would become an opioid addict – not just someone who takes opioids for pain, but someone who lives for her next fix. As much as I demanded, pleaded and protested, the boys wouldn't follow my directions.

Early the next morning, I awakened from that night of disturbing dreams. In their jumbled up way, I believe the nightmares conspired to bring me to an epiphany. If pain was to be my constant companion, then I would have to manage it through prayer and non-drug therapy. The narcotics would have to stop.

CHAPTER 28

Incarcerated

None of the doctors could give me a timeline for how long I was going to be incarcerated, and yes, I do mean "incarcerated," right there at Villa Rancho Bernardo. As wonderful a facility as it was, it might as well have been the slammer for me. And adding to the prison sentence was my having no idea how long I would be in rehab. I had the unfortunate duty of getting this poor, rebuilt body up for breakfast every morning, then pulling myself together enough so that a PT or an OT could help dress me and transfer me into a wheelchair because I hadn't yet learned to walk again. He or she then rolled me down to the gymnasium. It was the most up-to-date, magnificently-equipped gymnasium that I have ever seen. It was my personal torture chamber. And I have Cameron to thank for that!

I'd scan the room, looking at those diabolical machines with dread while I thought, "All right, what portion of Purgatory will I visit today?" And for almost three hours, six days a week, I lifted weights, pulled on levers, pushed on pedals and tried to stand on a mat with bars at hip level, desperately holding on as I took each excruciatingly painful step. And the next step. And the step after that. The course was 15 feet long, but it felt like 15 miles. It was Hell on Earth. I never thought I would learn to walk again. The pain was so intense that I wanted to give up and lie in bed with my opiate pills. But the therapy team would have none of that.

It seemed to take forever, yet with their encouragement, I did exactly what every one of those phenomenal gym experts wanted of me. They knew how tough it was for me – how incredibly painful each demand was, and how I loathed every critical hour of therapy.

Seven long weeks into therapy, I awakened early one Sunday morning to the sound of a gentle whisper, "PRICELESS!" At 4:30 in the morning, it was unbelievably frightening. I garnered my courage to turn on the light. Nobody was there. I waited a few minutes, thinking somebody would come into the room. Nobody did.

With all the steel rods in my body, I couldn't turn my head, so I desperately reached with my uninjured arm over my body to feel if someone was standing behind me. But nobody was there. Suddenly, I heard another whisper, "You are one of my precious children and I will always love you. You are priceless!" After all this time, The Almighty finally answered my question about the value of my life. I was comforted, realizing that even though it took almost two months, God had spoken to me. I felt safe and secure, turned off the light and drifted back to sleep.

A most exquisite dream

Soon after, I had the most amazing dream where The Almighty floated over to my mother, who had gone to Heaven 13 years earlier. She was sitting on the edge of her white, puffy cloud, weeping uncontrollably. She said, "Lord, my daughter is dying. She's too young. She has so much left to give and so much work to do on Earth. She's screaming out for your help."

The Almighty gently floated over to my mother's puffy cloud, sat down and smiled. God answered, "Not to worry, Doc. It's not my plan to take your daughter, yet. She must fulfill her worldly purpose. Besides, she has much to live for. Your daughter will soon become a grandmother. And you, Doc, will become a great-grandmother. So chin up and dry those tears." He gently smoothed her beautiful, silver glittery wings, gave my mom a hug and floated away.

When I awakened from that dream, I began to believe the content of those visions and the messages from the Holy Spirit. My life began to regain its meaning. I knew then and there that I'd return to be the person I'm supposed to be. And who knew when another precious little one might arrive?

Progress report

In the third month of physical therapy, the head of rehab. proudly showed me my progress chart.

"Mrs. Cramer, at first, you couldn't bend your leg more than two inches," she told me. "Now, look what you're able to do. From your knee down, you have a bending range of six inches!" I WAS healing!

I had graduated from wheelchair to walker when a therapist said, "Mrs. Cramer, I have a surprise for you. We are going to walk outside." Except for ambulance transfers, I hadn't been outside in over seven months. Hobbling through the Villa's front doors on my walker, I took in a view of gorgeous blue skies, billowy white clouds, lush greenery, colorful flowers and butterflies in the roses. But better than all the sights was the richly fragrant scent of nature. Warmth embraced every part of my body and I was startled to realize it was the middle of summer.

Very slowly, as I clung to my walker with my therapist at my side, we made our way around the entire perimeter of Villa Rancho Bernardo. I couldn't look up because of the steel rods in my neck, but I could see straight ahead and experience the sunshine and absolute euphoria of being outside. The tears were streaming down my face. My therapist asked, "Mrs. Cramer, are you all right?"

"I'm more than all right," I said. "I am alive!" I knew then and there that I would have the strength, patience and confidence to recover.

In the gym, through the pain, through the anguish, through the hours and hours of exercising, with the incredible compassion of all of my therapists and the generosity and kindness of my nurses and CNAs, the staff slowly saw my personality change. I became the lady that I used to be before the accident. But make no mistake – without the sympathetic caring staff at Villa Rancho Bernardo, you would not be reading this story.

One fine day, Cameron spirited me away for my first social outing since the accident. He got permission from the head rehab nurse to take me to lunch at my favorite restaurant, the Poseidon in Del Mar. We dined outside and as soon as our meals arrived, Cameron's cell phone went off. It was a call from his lovely wife, Katie, who had just come from the obstetrician's office.

"It's a boy, Cameron," she exclaimed. "We're going to have a baby boy!" I can't do justice by describing Cameron's expression as he listened to Katie's joyful news, but it was a miraculous combination of the wonder, pride and jubilation that only an expectant parent can convey. And very importantly, my prophetic dream that I was going to be a grandmother had come true!

CHAPTER 29

Wall of Healing

It has taken months of anguish and stubbornness, but I don't take opioids anymore. Randall helped a lot with this. These days, to manage my pain, I do water aerobics for about an hour every day in my back yard pool and walk Miramar Lake with girlfriends. I have an everlasting "Attitude of Gratitude" and realize how blessed I am to still be here.

But that's getting ahead of the story. I was still at Villa Rancho Bernardo and dealing with rehab and medical bill worries. Thank God I married a commander in the Navy because I have TRICARE insurance that, fortunately, covered most of my bills.

My boys were so compassionate when they came to visit me. They were overjoyed that I was still alive. They had tears in their eyes, but held it together, because I – who was always the strong one – was in such a fragile state. The boys sorted through my get-well cards and taped them to the wall facing my bed. I awakened each day to a gorgeous collage of hummingbirds, butterflies, waterfalls and flowers on the cards I received from my friends and family. They continually brought me a variety of helium balloons for every holiday – Valentine's Day, St. Patrick's Day, Easter, Mother's Day, Memorial Day, Fourth of July and Labor Day. They taped these to the wall, too, adding to the color and dimension of the room, along with marking the slow passage of time. So, when I got that horrid wake-up call with the flashing lights at 6:45 a.m., I would sit up and look over those stunning symbols of life and know I would one day leave rehab. It became my Wall of Healing.

I pushed myself to my limits and sweated bullets on those torturous machines every single day except Sunday. Those workouts hurt like hell. I cried bitter tears every day from the excruciating pain. Sundays were my day of rest. Of course, the gym was closed on the Sabbath, so I couldn't have worked out even if I'd wanted to. Which I didn't.

From the repeated heparin blood thinner shots, my abdomen became a veritable dark rainbow of bruises – blue, green, purple, brown and black. My belly was a place of stabbing pain all the time. Yet despite the shots, there was always the risk that I'd develop another blood clot. After the accident, there were so many shattered places in my body where my blood clotted, I had an extensive series of deep vein thromboses and pulmonary embolisms. I was a prime candidate for a clot to float through my body, up through my femoral vein and land anywhere it liked. I was concerned that I might die from a deadly blockage racing into my brain, the same process that took my beloved mother's life.

The day the staff greeted me with the surprising news that I was to be released in 10 days, I got incredibly excited. Suddenly, I experienced a severe pain that devoured all the joy in the room. I punched my hospital help button. I turned bright red and my gym suit became soaked with sweat. I screamed in agony because I couldn't stand the pain. I was immediately ambulanced to Conrad Prebys Cardiovascular Institute. The cardiologist discovered a blood clot had lodged in the lower lobe of my right lung. Hailing back to my battle with breast cancer, when I'd endured radiation and chemotherapy, the aggressive rays burned the lower lobe of my right lung. I've had a lot of trouble breathing because I don't have complete lung capacity. I live with COPD. That's precisely where this newest coagulated bloody mass landed – in the most vulnerable part of my body. After a five-day struggle, the dedicated physicians successfully decreased the clot and overcame the threat to my life. Once again, I am forever grateful to the magnanimous Conrad Prebys.

Home Sweet Home

The day of discharge came not a moment too soon. The facility director, all the wonderful doctors, CNAs, OTs, and PTs surprised me with a very special farewell party. They provided a cake with teal icing – my favorite color – and a lovely celebration. Hugging them all, I told them how much I appreciated their care for and about me. I was humbled by their compassion and life-saving attention. After a tearful good-bye, Cameron joyfully drove me to my home in Scripps Ranch.

I laid eyes on my cherished residence for the first time in 10 months. After everything – after the struggles to put Humpty Dumpty back together again – I was home to my forever sanctuary. As we pulled into the driveway, I cried happy tears and three words came to mind.

"Home Sweet Home."

CHAPTER 30

Only the Good Die Young

In the spring of my first year back home, Cameron came over to say, "Mom, you've been in this house all by yourself for almost eight months, so I've got a great idea. I know you love Billy Joel."

"I adore Billy Joel!" I exclaimed.

He responded, "Well, Billy Joel is going to be doing a concert Mother's Day weekend."

I said, "Fabulous! Where? What playhouse?" He responded, "It's not going to be at a playhouse, Mom. It's going to be downtown at Petco Park where the Padres play. There'll be 59,000 of his 'nearest and dearest' in attendance. I'll get us tickets. I want to take you to hear Billy Joel live and in concert."

"Cameron, that would be the most phenomenal Mother's Day gift ever!" I exclaimed. When Mother's Day weekend arrived, we drove to the enormous stadium. We parked and found the way to our seats in the bleachers. There were two enormous video screens — that's where I caught my first glimpse of Billy Joel. He took the microphone and I heard the voice of one of my musical heroes. He spoke very briefly: "Thank you all, we appreciate you coming out, we know it's a big weekend." And then Billy Joel started singing. I sank down in my seat and went to another world.

The third tune he sang has always been one of my favorites. It's called, "Only the Good Die Young." After he sang it, I looked over to Cameron and joked, "See, Cameron? I guess I'm not really very good, 'because I'm still here." My son laughed.

When Billy Joel finished the song to thunderous applause, I needed to stretch my legs. With great difficulty, I stood up. I glanced at Cameron and remarked, "Sweetheart, in that song, my favorite lyrics are, 'I'd rather laugh with the sinners than cry with the saints. The sinners are much more fun.'" I turned around and announced to everybody within earshot, "You want to know something? It would have been okay if God hadn't let me live. I'll tell you right now. I would've gone down to Hell and Satan and I would still be partying." With that, I turned back around and sat down next to my son. All the people who heard me burst into laughter. Cameron stood, turned around, looked down at me, then he looked up and said, "Ladies and gentlemen, I have absolutely no idea who this woman is." I still remember the laughter.

Given the reaction from the crowd, and Cameron's generosity, that concert was one of the most memorable musical events in my life. Now, let me tell you about another one.

Cameron took me to the Billy Joel concert in the spring of 2016 for Mother's Day. What fun being out in public again!

Calling all angels

I love the internationally-renowned band Train. Lead singer Patrick Monahan is one of my all-time favorite recording artists. In the midst of my coma, in addition to Randall's and Cameron's whispers of *"Nil Desperandum"* and their ocean sounds CD, my fabulous nurses would play a phenomenal Train album. To me, "Calling All Angels" is a particularly meaningful song. I believe that somehow, I heard Pat Monahan singing those words directly to me.

I have been quite involved with a variety of many child abuse prevention charities here in San Diego for almost 30 years. They include Voices for Children, Angels Foster Family, Center for Community Solutions, Home Start, Casa de Amparo, Vista Hill and Walden Family Services. I have a special place in my heart for all of them. Walden Family Services has always invited me to their annual gala, "Dream On." The CEO, Tanya Terosian, is a good friend. When she told me that their 2019 entertainment was to be Train, I was beside myself! After dinner and both the silent and live auctions, with my very good friends from *Ranch and Coast Magazine,* I made my way to the front of the ballroom to listen to the band's fabulous music.

Train took the stage. Pat Monohan started singing. Their fifth number was none other than "Calling All Angels." Suddenly, I realized that was the song played for me while I was in my coma. I looked up at Pat and started crying. I was dressed to the nines for that event, but emotion overcame me and I didn't care that tears were destroying my makeup. I slowly and subtly inched toward the stage. I then crawled up on this huge three and a half foot speaker, with stockings and heels (Dr. Thunder, I hope you're not reading this. He was my orthopedic surgeon – chief of orthopedic surgery at Scripps Memorial Hospital Trauma Center, La Jolla – who saved my right leg from amputation following the accident. He said, "Mrs. Cramer, under no circumstances am I ever to see you wearing heels.") Dr. Thunder wasn't there that night, so I was good to go.

As I clambered up on the stage, the security guard in the back grabbed his gun, moved forward a few steps and I gave him the "Hey, not to worry" sign. I moved a little closer to Patrick at the front of the stage. At that point, the singing star spied me and looked at me a little askance, as if to say, "What in the world is this crazy woman doing on my stage?"

I cautiously walked over to Patrick and whispered in his ear, "This will only take a minute. I think you'll find it worthwhile." He relinquished the mic and I said, "Ladies and gentlemen, my husband and I were killed four years ago. My husband succumbed to his injuries. I died too, but the Lord said, 'No, we're not ready for her, yet. She has too much left to do on Earth.' So God sent me back.

"It took me three months in a medically induced coma and six months of rehab to come back to the lady I used to be. And one of the main reasons I am here is because my precious nurses at Scripps Memorial Hospital played 'Calling All Angels' while I was unconscious. I remember every word. I had not heard that song in more than four years. But hearing that song this evening, I was moved to climb up on the stage to tell Patrick and every single one of you that one of the reasons I am standing here before you is because of Train. And because of Patrick. And because of 'Calling All Angels.'"

With that, the audience showed its approval with applause and cheers. The security guard kindly put his gun away, and helped me off the back of the stage so I wouldn't have to scramble down the speaker.

The concert wound down and Tanya awaited to drive me back home. As we readied to leave, a large gathering of patrons surrounded me, holding my hand, hugging me and exclaiming, "We had no idea what you've been through. We have been so moved and inspired by your story. Thank you for your impromptu sharing!" I think even Pat was pleased.

Excerpt from Train's
Calling All Angels

I need a sign,
to let me know you're here
All of these lines are being crossed over
the atmosphere I need to know, that
things are gonna look up
'Cause I feel us drowning
in a sea spilled from a cup
When there is no place safe
and no safe place to put my head When
you can feel the world shake from the
words that are said
And I-I-I-I'm,
calling all angels...

And I won't give up, if
you don't give up I
won't give up...

CHAPTER 31

Tragedy to Triumph

It's been a long, evolving, life-changing awakening. Excruciating, unbelievable, at times funny and absolutely inexplicable. I'm grateful to have survived. In discovering how much I have loved, and how much I've learned about what's really important in this world, my family, my friends and my charities – this journey has reinforced in me the principle of paying it forward by giving back.

Mine has been a discovery of patience and perseverance, of traveling through the pain and recognizing the faces of the ones who have been there for me – the number of people it took to carry me and walk with me along this course of discovery. The ones who have always been there, the new spirits of love who have offered support and guidance for segments or the entirety of my specialized care. These powerful people didn't just save my life. They brought the life within me forward. I have returned to share my life with my cherished sons Randall and Cameron, my incredible daughter-in-law, Katie, and my precious grandchildren Liam and Selena Grace.

Cameron, my grandchildren Liam and Selena Grace, and daughter-in-law Katie

I have reclaimed my southern steel magnolia roots. I continue to experience the joy of witnessing my sons' successes in life. I am thrilled that my granddaughter carries on my powerful family legacy as the fifth generation of Graces. It is beyond wonderful to still be alive. I have a great and humbling sense of gratitude, and frankly, material things mean virtually nothing to me. Most importantly, I've never been closer to The Almighty.

Indeed, I have come full circle from tragedy to triumph. I am not only surviving. I am thriving.

Gigi's grandchildren love their play dates and just plain spending time with their Grammy.

CHAPTER 32

My Sons

The elder son, by Randall Hawkins Schiff

Mom tells me that as her firstborn, I was the first one to teach her to be a mother. In turn, she taught me about faith in God, integrity, sincerity, honesty and hard work – the same lessons passed down to her from my grandmother.

My fondest memories of growing up are our family vacations. The fact that Mom, a single parent, was able to take us boys on vacations at all, is not lost on me. It couldn't have been easy for her with two rambunctious children to look after, but she made fun happen for us. We traveled to places like Hawaii, where we went snorkeling and parasailing. Or she'd take us to Mexico where we would buy fireworks and we'd have a blast (so to speak) under her watchful eye. She took us someplace special every year.

She also drove us up to Disneyland where Cameron and I got to spend a whole day riding all the rides. Gigi joined us on some of the more tame attractions when we were little, like the Teacups and A Small World. But as we got older and took on the extreme features, she'd let us go off on our own and be waiting for us at the exit of each roller coaster.

Randall, age 9, 1987

She also bought annual passes to Sea World, where we'd spend all day. Mom loved the ocean and all ocean life. This was a place where she could safely share that passion with us. She'd come with us to see various sea critters or Shamu. Then, with an armful of magazines, she sat reading while Cameron and I tore it up at Captain Kidd's World.

By virtue of example, Mom ingrained a powerful work ethic in my brother and me. As a single mother trying to put food on the table, she had to spend a lot of time working. To cover for her when she was gone, she hired live-ins to care for us. But she was always there for us when we needed her and to cheer us on at our sporting and school events.

Christianity was a large part of our life growing up. She always took us to church and Sunday School when we were little. Later on, she sent us to Christian retreats at the JH Ranch in Etna, California. I have great memories from those retreats, too. The place provided valuable Bible lessons mixed in with a whole lot of fun.

When I grew up, I followed Mom and my stepfather into their professional world. I'm proud to say that my stepfather was the president of the California Association of Realtors (CAR) and Mom was the top agent in her office. Also, my father was a broker and my step-mother, a realtor. It just made sense to me to follow in their footsteps. I became a licensed realtor in 2007.

The day of the accident, I was jogging at the Torrey Pines State Reserve in Del Mar. I was an avid runner and had just finished my workout when I noticed a message on my phone. It was from an ICU nurse at Scripps Hospital. The message informed me my parents had been in a car accident and I needed to come there right away

I returned the hospital's call and was told they couldn't divulge specifics over the phone. I just needed to get there right away. Of course, I jumped in my car and headed for the hospital, calling my brother on the way. He'd gotten the same call and was on his way there, too. We met up in the ER and when a social worker took us into a little private conference room, we knew it was really serious. They told us our stepfather had passed. That was jarring, but when I asked how my mom was, the social worker just kind of cringed. Then a doctor arrived to deliver the news. It wasn't good.

Mom was in surgery for God knows how long. Afterwards, I didn't want to see her all beaten and bruised. I was pretty shaken up, probably in shock. Cameron and his wife, Katie, went in. When they returned, Cameron said, "Man, you need to see Mom." So I gathered up my courage and went into the ICU. It was horrible. Mom's legs were so swollen and she was lying there with all these machines, wires and tubes hooked into her. She barely resembled the strong and vibrant woman who had raised me. I broke down and soon, as a survival technique, I became numb and kind of went to a different place in my mind.

After her many surgeries and she was stabilized, I never left Mom's side. But 24-7 in an ICU, especially when Mom was completely out of it, became too exhausting. And futile, for that matter, because we couldn't do anything for her. Then Cameron and I developed a routine to make sure at least one of us would be with her every day. After the swelling and bruising in her face subsided, there were times when we could pretend she was just sleeping.

The surgeons remarked that this was about the worst car accident they'd ever seen. I didn't think she would make it. If she did live, we worried she would end up like Christopher Reeve, the actor who became so disabled. But we did as Mom taught us — we never gave up hope. Every time before I left, I'd kiss her on the cheek or the forehead or wherever there wasn't a tube, and I would say our family motto – "NIL DESPERANDUM."

To escape our worries after hospital visits, we'd stop at Jersey Mike's for a sandwich and hit the beach in Del Mar for some surfing. Meanwhile, I started researching what happens to patients who have extended ICU care. I discovered a condition called IC psychosis and realized Mom would face some tough times when she woke up. I was ready for it — the hallucinations, the paranoia, all of it. What none of us was prepared for was withdrawal from all the medications, like anti-depressants, cholesterol pills, heart medication and, most significantly, opioids. At first, she probably needed the latter because she was in so much pain. But by the time she got to rehab, they were giving her too much of it.

When Mom understood she was being over-medicated, she was infuriated. She insisted she didn't need those drugs in her system and stopped taking the majority of them cold turkey. To help mitigate the serious symptoms of opioid leaving her bloodstream, I bought her chocolate covered blueberry medical marijuana edibles. Obtaining and using cannabis for medical reasons was legal by then, but Villa Rancho Bernardo management didn't want patients to have food or medications brought in from the outside. So I hid the edibles inside the Kleenex box next to her bed. The sweets helped take her mind off her horrible pain and intense drug withdrawal symptoms. Those little edibles were our best tool in helping Mom get over oxycodone dependence. It took some doing, but she conquered it.

While Mom was recovering, I handled the details of running her household, like paying the pool and gardening guys, doing basic maintenance and collecting her mail. When it was clear she would come home with walking disabilities, I had a stairlift installed in her house. I also retrofitted her bathroom to

Miracle Warrior

make it "handicapable" – not handicapped – accessible, including redesigning her shower so she could sit down.

When Mom came home, I put my professional career on hold and moved into her house for a year to be her caregiver. To expedite her road to recovery, I cooked and provided healthy meals to give her the best quality of life possible. I studied dietician books, took her to all of her doctor appointments, and aided in the research of her orthopedic prosthetics so critical for her to walk properly, because her femur had been shattered, resulting in one of her legs being shorter than the other one.

I wasn't obligated to do all this. Instead, I felt entrusted to help the most important woman in my life. Still, I maintained my real estate license and nowadays, do property management and also work for Amazon as an independent contractor.

The car wreck was the easy part – the road to recovery is the lifelong journey! But every single day, she's getting better and stronger.

The younger son, by Cameron Crockett Schiff

I have known no one in my life but my mom as a parent. She has been able to be not only the best mother a son could ask for but I never felt that I was missing a father. She was there for everything, whether volunteering in my classroom and giving me extra flashcard time or taking me to soccer games and cheering me on for every goal I scored. Mom always encouraged a healthy lifestyle and it led me to find an interest in running. She even drove me to school early every morning so I could run laps before my class started. We also enjoyed playing tennis together frequently. We had a blast during our local Senior - Sprouts Tennis tournaments, in which we were often the champions.

Cameron, age 6, 1987

Mom was my rock whom I could and still turn to whenever I need anything. I consider myself the luckiest son on the planet because I can still hug my mom. She's still here and thriving. As strong as our bond was prior to the life-shattering accident, we are even closer now.

137

She wasn't necessarily strict, but she gave us boundaries. If we pushed the line too far, she'd rein us in. Very importantly, she trusted us. My brother and I tried our best not to violate that trust.

I was at home with my wife, Katie, when I got the worst phone call of my life. It's strange how your life can be altered so drastically from one call. The nurse said, "Your parents have been in a car accident. You need to get here right away. That's all I can tell you over the phone." She hung up and I began to panic. I called Randall and let him know we needed to get to the hospital immediately. Upon our arrival, some of our family members were already there and nervously awaiting news.

It was nearly two nerve-racking hours before we were updated. Dr. Dandan and a social worker came into a small waiting room. As gently as he could, the doctor said, "We performed life-saving techniques on Commander Edward Cramer for over an hour. Unfortunately, we could not save him." My heart sank. As much as I loved Ed, I thought, "Oh, no. What about Mom?"

Dr. Dandan then explained that "Grace [Gigi] is currently critically stable. We had to perform numerous surgeries to keep her alive."

Good as his word, Cameron graduated valedictorian of his PIMA Medical Institute class in 2018.

Hours later, she was stabilized enough that we could see her. Randall opted out, which I understood. We each handled the tragedy in different ways. Although it was the hardest thing I'd ever done, I walked down a long hall to where my mother lay. I found her in a medically-induced coma, intubated and being kept alive by machines. The damaged and destroyed, bloody and broken body in front of me couldn't possibly be that same athletic fearless leader who was spelunking in caves with me in Mexico two weeks prior. Unfortunately, over the next three months in the hospital, six months in rehab and day by day after her being discharged home, we came to realize that this was, in fact, our new post-accident reality.

We'd been told that Mom had about a 4 percent chance of survival, to which I responded, "You don't know my mother. She's a fighter. She's going to pull through." The first six weeks Mom was hospitalized, every single day, I woke up not knowing if she was going to come out of it. The doctors kept telling us, "She's critically stable." That basically meant, "She can turn at any minute."

We had a few scares along the way. One time, she coded, which is medical jargon for going into cardiac or respiratory arrest. Again, Randall and I rushed to the hospital. But my feisty mother overcame.

They say there are no atheists in foxholes. I'm not necessarily religious, but I am spiritual. I believe in a higher power and I did pray. I made a deal with God – If Mom recovered, I promised that I would rededicate my life to saving lives.

Throughout the ordeal, I witnessed the class and professionalism of Scripps' doctors, CNAs, nurses, and respiratory therapists – every single one of them giving her 100 percent. It was phenomenal. With their help, Mom rallied and I made good on my end of the deal. I'm now a respiratory therapist. After extensive education, because I have the utmost respect for Scripps Memorial Hospital, I applied for a position there and was hired.

While Randall took care of Mom's home, I researched a rehab facility for the next phase of her recovery. Still, we didn't know how much mobility she'd have. We hoped for the best, but feared the worst. It was a good 15 months before I was confident she was going to recover.

Prior to the accident, my brother and I had a pretty good relationship. But I was married and focusing on being a family man and we grew a little distant. After the accident, we became as close as we had ever been. We bonded over the accident and one of our coping mechanisms after going to visit Mom in the hospital was surfing. I remember one day, Randall and I were at the beach after a day with Mom. It was storming and getting dark. Frankly, those were very treacherous, dangerous conditions, not to mention the fact that we were surfing in February in the heart of winter without wetsuits. The waves were eight- to ten-footers. It was insane! We were kind of numb to the pain of everything. We looked at each other and one of us said, "We need this." We grabbed our boards and went out in the ocean. It was extremely liberating, knowing that anything could happen at any moment, but we were enjoying it, living life to the fullest, just as Mom always taught us. Knowing how much Mom loves the ocean, I made a recording of the waves and would ensure that it was playing constantly during her ICU stay.

When I met my wife, one thing that attracted me to her was her very personable ways. She was energetic, friendly and loved meeting people. That's the way Mom is. Fortunately for me, Katie and my mom get along extremely well. Katie definitely appreciates Mom, and we're so grateful that she is still here to be a Grammy to our two children. We realize how close we were to losing her. But it's like we have a new lease on life with Mom.

Our kids, Liam and Selena Grace, love their "Grammy." They always want to go see her and play with her. And more importantly, Grammy can't wait to go on daily adventures to the zoo or Sea World with them.

My wife, Katie, is an ICU trauma nurse. During Mom's ICU stay, Katie was the interpreter/liaison among the nurses, doctors, Randall and me. She made sure we understood the medical lingo that was being spoken. Katie, knowing how important it is for medical staff to know who their patients are, made certain that they knew Mom. She posted several large photos near Mom's bed of our entire family spelunking near Tulum, Mexico, just two weeks before the accident. The nurses could hardly believe that the shattered, broken woman lying in the ICU bed was that same vigorous, strong and courageous woman exploring the caves of Mexico. Through Randall's and my daily visits, and Katie's extra efforts, everyone in that hospital knew how powerful Mom was, and how much she was loved.

I truly believe that we have a miracle family and that Mom is a Miracle Warrior.

Making friends with a gentle giant in Baja California's LAGUNA SAN IGNACIO, February 2020 (just before COVID shut the world down)

Acknowledgements

How do I even begin to acknowledge all the amazing people who have been and are so important in my life, and in my recovery back to living after the car crash? I suppose the best place to begin is where I have always started – with The Almighty. Of course, there is my phenomenal Mother, who helped shape me into the woman I became. Then there are my incredible sons, Randall and Cameron, my daughter-in-law, Katie, and two extraordinary grandchildren, Liam and Selena Grace. Next comes my second husband, whose love and devotion opened up the entire world to me and gave me an incredibly deeper meaning to my life.

I would be remiss if I didn't thank Ed McShane, who in 2020 became a friend as he spent hours with me, recording my remarks and transcribing/editing those interviews. Thanks, also, to my associate writers, editors and designers, Christina M. Cavitt and Geni Cavitt of Cavitt Productions. Additionally, I am indebted to the talented medical professionals at Scripps Memorial Hospital and Villa Rancho Bernardo Rehabilitation Center who brought me back to life and cared for me during my recovery. Also, I'm grateful to Dr. Clair Berry & his wife, Charlotte, as well as Reverend Ken Huff, who visited me at Villa Rancho Bernardo regularly, the many members of Torrey Pines Christian Church whose prayers sustained me, and my closest friends who called on me frequently while I was "incarcerated," and still stand beside me on this continuing journey. Finally, I am grateful to *Ranch & Coast* magazine for its assistance in finding resources to help me write my story. You know who you are and God bless you for being there. You have given me the compassion, support and love that have brought me through from tragedy to triumph.

I am also compelled to mention the many organizations and institutions which I have compassionately supported with my prayers and donations every year:

- American Association of University Women (AAUW)
- Angels Foster Family Network
- ASPCA (American Society for the Prevention of Cruelty to Animals)
- Casa de Amparo
- Center for Community Solutions
- Chi Omega Sorority
- College of William & Mary
- Colonial Williamsburg Foundation
- Country Friends
- Dorris Howell Foundation
- Environmental Defense Fund
- Greenpeace
- Helen Woodward Animal Center
- Home Start
- Hubbs-Seaworld Research Institute
- Just In Time
- KPBS
- Lambs Players Theatre
- Make-A-Wish Foundation
- Miracle Babies
- New Village Arts Theatre
- North Coast Repertory Theatre
- Ocean Conservancy International
- Old Globe Theatre
- Promises2Kids
- St. Germaine Children's Charity
- Salvation Army
- San Diego Crew Classic Regatta
- Sanford Burnham Prebys Medical Discovery Institute
- Scripps Memorial Hospital, La Jolla
- Torrey Pines Christian Church
- USO (United Services Organizations)
- Vista Hill Foundation
- Voices For Children
- Walden Family Services
- World Wildlife Fund
- Wounded Warrior Project

Gigi Cramer, long-term Champion for Sea Change, with her two grandchildren whale watching off the coast of San Diego.

I am devoted to all of my charitable organizations. Because of my strong support for keeping our oceans pristine and our planet as clean as possible, I've been appointed one of the *Champions for Sea Change* with Ocean Conservancy International. I was thrilled when they took this whale watching picture last January of me and my grandchildren, Liam and Selena Grace, with Hubbs-SeaWorld Research Institute. Loving the oceans and having been scuba diving for 30+ years, I was so honored to be part of Ocean Conservancy's 2020 Annual Report.

In addition to this list are some 20 other charities such as Best Friends, Alaska Raptor Center, Planned Parenthood and AARP. Their endeavors make the world a better place. I am humbled beyond words to be associated with all these fine people, organizations and institutions. In my family, we offer what we call the *La La La La La* Toast, which means "To Life, Love, Laughter, Liberty and Longevity" and I lift my glass to you all… no matter what color the wine is!

Finally, I appreciate you, dear reader. I hope you buckled up and had a wild ride right along with me. Thank you for reading my story.

Gigi at her pool, where she continues swimming as part of her daily therapy.

(Photo courtesy of Ranch & Coast Magazine)

ABOUT CAVITT PRODUCTIONS

Cavitt sisters Christina and Geni grew up in Richfield, Minnesota, and come from a long line of storytellers. When their grandmother and great aunts came to visit, they wove exciting 'olden-day' tales for all of the Cavitt children, especially impressing the girls. At dinnertime, their advertising executive dad regaled the family with escapades of his trade in the Minneapolis-St. Paul business arena.

As they grew up, they learned to tell stories, too. Eventually, Geni moved west to work in San Diego radio and television. Christina stayed in the Midwest to write business communications and biographies.

They discovered how well their myriad talents blended when they teamed up to create a photo-video legacy project in 2009. They had so much fun that they continued to work together, playing to one another's strengths. Their small-but-mighty company features a wealth of writing, voice over, photography, design, publishing and video experience.

Please visit www.CavittProductions.com for more information.

CPSIA information can be obtained
at www.ICGtesting.com
Printed in the USA
BVHW020328130422
634069BV00013BA/887

9 781662 922350